# MY KIND OF HEROES
## NOT THE USUAL KIND—BOOK ONE

## BY CARL DOUGLASS

Neurosurgeon Turned Author Writes With Gripping Realism

PUBLICATION
CONSULTANTS
WE BELIEVE IN THE POWER OF AUTHORS

PO Box 221974 Anchorage, Alaska 99522-1974
books@publicationconsultants.com—www.publicationconsultants.com

ISBN 978-1-63747-399-3
eISBN 978-1-63747-400-6


Library of Congress Catalog Card Number: 2024938076



Copyright 2024 Carl Douglass
—First Edition—

Manufactured in the United States of America.

# Dedication

To the publisher of my books, Evan Swensen, the staff of Publication Consultants, and the brilliant members of Author Masterminds, my friends and mentors.

# Disclaimer

This book—one of seven–is nonfiction and presents brief historical snippets about heroes—the unsung kind. In my opinion, there are almost no sports, movie, television, or comic book characters—often mislabeled as heroes. Not everyone will agree with my choices and omissions, but I hope even my detractors will find these people interesting or even inspiring. The criteria for selection include relative anonymity; the famous presidential and kingly military warriors and major historical figures have already had adequate coverage. These people's histories also deserve attention.

CNN has a yearly selection of marvelous people who are rightly considered to be heroes because of the great good they do. I agree with the designation for those people, and every one of them could be featured here. But CNN has taken care of that very well. Actually, several of my choices of heroes are well known and receive homage in their own countries, but they deserve a more general amount of approbation, so here it is.

# Adam Freestone 1989 to the Present

Adam Freestone is the author's friend, and it could be possible that Carl Douglass is biased in placing Mr. Freestone—33 years old at the time of this writing—in my book of heroes. Once his story is told, I am sure no one will doubt the appropriateness of the choice.

Adam was born December 18, 1989, to Arden Freestone and Kathleen Freestone in Roosevelt, Utah. He is—like many in his birthplace—an active member of the Church of Jesus Christ of latter-day Saints. He has a sister Ashley, eight years older than him, a brother Justin, five years older, and a sister Randi two years younger.

Roosevelt is a small town 141 miles southeast of Salt Lake City. Roosevelt was a truck farming, ranching, and cowboy, town, population 3915 at the time. It grew at about 1000 per year. It was 80% White, 6,3%American Indian, and 0.2% persons with a disability.

A bit of history of Roosevelt: it is a small city/town situated in Duchesne County on US Route 40 in the northeast corner of the state, south of the Uinta Mountains, at an elevation of 5,250 feet. It is located 141 miles southeast of Salt Lake City, 30 miles east of the small town of Vernal, and 28 miles west of the smaller town of Duchesne.

In 1861, Abraham Lincoln, President of the United States–by proclamation–set aside a reservation for the Ute Indian Nation. No survey was made beforehand; it had merely a general description as comprising all the lands from the tops of the mountains to the north to the tops of the mountains to the south draining into what later was defined as the Duchesne River.

The area thus set apart was vast. It was larger than some of the states of the Union and larger than some of the nations of the world. A few Nomadic

Indians, government employees, and some Episcopalian Missionaries, were the only inhabitants of the area to begin with.

Lincoln's proclamation created the setting for another land rush, perhaps the same as the great Oklahoma rush on September 16, 1893. Fortunately–in the Big "U" Country–the red tape made the rush much more orderly. Still, the homesteaders came by the hundreds.

An old Ute said, "When the Americats came they came by the many manys. They came nose to tail like a string of black ants crossing the sand."

Some came from Colorado through Vernal, some through Strawberry Valley, but most came along the stage road from Price through Nine Mile Canyon.

An old timer who lived at the Strip (Gusher) before and during "the opening" said, "it was like the touch of a fairy's wand; yesterday there was nothing but wilderness and desert; today there are fences, ditches, plowing, plantings, houses, and towns; settlers were everywhere... it was almost magical."

Ed Harmston was the unanimously agreed upon founder of Roosevelt City. It was said that Ed F. Harmston was an enigma. He was an engineer and mathematician on one hand and a dreamer on the other. Exactly when he founded Roosevelt City, no one knows for sure. However, way out in the middle of nowhere was a small, flat-topped mesa overshadowed by a higher bench to the west. Nothing grew there but shad scale, rabbit brush, and desert grass. There was a prairie dog town in the center and wild horses grazed across it every day. The little bench had one dry gulch on one side flanked by another dry gulch on the other. The nearest stream of running water was miles away.

Harmston knew the country like the back of his hand. He had surveyed part of it long before the opening, yet in spite of his knowledge; he chose that dry little desert bench for his homestead claim. His choice was one of planning or dreaming, or a little of both. Harmston was more of a doer than a talker.

Under the Proclamation law, you picked your land and paid $2.25 an acre for one hundred and sixty acres. You then had to move on the land, build an abode, improve it, and live there five years. After you "proved up," you received title in "fee simple" by way of a patent from the US government. Harmston made his entry and paid his money, but he was too busy a man to move on and make improvements. He erected a boarded-up tent and installed his two sons A.C. (Craig) and Floyd (Nick) Harmston to begin living out his time for him. These sons were the very first residents of Roosevelt, Utah.

A.C. Harmston said, "Early one morning, father showed up with all his surveying equipment; and we began that day to lay out the streets, alleys, and lots, of a town. I thought maybe my old man had been sun struck; and Nick knew darn well he had; but we kept on working day after day until the job was done."

The town was incorporated at a mass meeting of 44 citizens on February 21, 1913.

The Ute Indians were moved there when the Mormons settled the Wasatch Front, and there began to be wars between the white settlers and the indigenous Americans soon thereafter. As Utah grew, the Ute Reservation in the great Uintah Basin was opened to white settlers in 1905 and 1906 by an act of the US Congress.

Tragedy hovered over the Freestone family in the form of heritable Duchenne's Disease. Justin died in June, 2022, at age 38, of causes incident to the disease. Since his brother had it, and the disease is genetic and primarily affects males, it was practically guaranteed that Adam would have it. Adam was diagnosed with the disease in utero which was a harbinger of a tough life ahead. DMD [Duchenne muscular dystrophy] is a rare and severe genetic disorder that causes progressive muscle weakness and wasting.

Muscular dystrophy is a group of diseases that cause progressive weakness and loss of muscle mass. In muscular dystrophy, mutations [abnormal genes] interfere with the production of proteins needed to form healthy muscle. There are many kinds of muscular dystrophy. Symptoms of the most common variety begin in childhood, mostly in boys.

In Justin's case, the signs and symptoms began to be noticeable when he was five years old. For Adam, the diagnosis was made in utero. There is no cure for muscular dystrophy. However, medications and therapy can help manage symptoms and slow the course of the disease to a degree. Justin died of his disease at the age of 38, and Adam was quadriplegic and machine-dependent at age 33. He has a full-time aide to keep him alive and his brain and writing ability active.

Beginning very early, Adam showed pseudohypertrophy [hyper-development of the lower limbs and thinness of the arms], and lumbar hyperlordosis. DMD causes progressive muscle weakness due to muscle fiber disarray, death, and replacement with connective tissue or fat.

The main sign of muscular dystrophy, in general, is progressive muscle weakness. Specific signs and symptoms begin at different ages and in different muscle groups, depending on the type of muscular dystrophy. Duchenne-type muscular dystrophy is the most common form. Although girls can be carriers and mildly affected, it is far more common in boys.

Signs and symptoms—which typically appear in early childhood—may include frequent falls, difficulty rising from a lying or sitting position, trouble running and jumping, a waddling gait, walking on the toes, large calf muscles, muscle pain, and stiffness, learning disabilities, and delayed growth.

Certain genes are involved in making proteins that protect muscle fibers. Muscular dystrophy occurs when one of these genes is defective. DMD specifically is caused by mutations in *DMD* (encoding dystrophin) that prevent the production of the muscle isoform of dystrophin (Dp427m). The most common variety, Duchenne's, mostly occurs in young boys. People with a family history of muscular dystrophy are at a much higher risk of developing the disease or passing it on to their children, as was the case with Adam's mother. But it can be spontaneous in a given individual.

The complications of progressive muscle weakness appear at varying ages, usually in early boyhood, and with variable severity and timing of progression. However, the muscle cells that are replaced by fat cells, all become useless. So, as time goes on, the body loses more and more muscle and function eventually, most of the following complications present themselves, often in the following order: Adam suffered all of them except learning disability:

**Trouble walking**–most eventually need to use a wheelchair; Daily Living; limit mobility; breathing problems related to progressive weakness of the muscles associated with breathing. Most DMD patients, like

Adam, eventually need to use a ventilator, half starting at age 20. Adam's continuing existence depends on such a breathing assistance device; scoliosis–which are unable to hold the spine straight; heart efficiency of the heart muscle. If the muscles involved with swallowing are affected, nutritional problems and aspiration pneumonia can develop. Adam knows full well the experience of hospital stays for treatment; feeding tubes might be an option.

The two boys walked more slowly than the other children their age, then they had trouble standing. From there, it was a steady but far slower decline in muscle loss. Adam and Justin had to use wheelchairs ~age 10 due to weakening muscles. He and his brother were prone to injuries from falling while they were still walking. Justin once fell into a pumpkin growing in their grandparents' garden at a bad angle and broke his arm.

Justin first started using a power wheelchair after the family moved to Alaska [1995]. They lived in a ground-floor apartment with stairs to leave the Building; so, they were forced to store his wheelchair outside of the apartment. The boys' parents had to carry Justin out to it for him to use it. Life was becoming a dedication to the physical care of the two boys. Thankfully, they were able to move to a house shortly afterward.

The disease progressed; and the parents, sisters, and the boys, had to adjust accordingly. They used their motorized wheelchairs successfully on flat floors, but there was the problem of stairs. They put in wheelchair stairs which worked for a time, but finally all small elevations in the household terrain became impassable objects. They had to put in ramps at the house to allow the boys full access. They made a quantum jump beyond using a manual lift to help with transferring them in and out of their chairs. They went right to a barrier free lift that hung from the ceiling. It was far less cumbersome than the manual systems. This, however, required the parents to install an expensive rail system in their ceiling; so, the lift had a track to sit in.

There remained the growing difficulty with transportation. It was apparent that they also needed to buy a vehicle that was capable of carrying wheelchairs. This is further complicated because both boys used a wheelchair and usually had to be transported together for visits and to see doctors. Adam's father was a truck driver in Utah; so, he wanted a diesel similar to what he was used to driving. He also wanted a vehicle that was almost guaranteed never to get stuck. This was probably totally unnecessary because the family was not really expecting to travel in terrain purposely that was overly rough.

Then for reasons that only he knew, Father Arden made it a raised van that was one or two feet higher than the same base model of the van. Adam figured that he wanted to make sure they were safe in the event of a car accident, because they could probably run over any vehicle that was involved. Snow was also a potential issue that went into his thinking presumably. Being frugal people, the family still has the same van; and 20+ years later it is still in good condition and still works. However, they did splurge for a more reasonably sized van for one wheelchair at a time in 2022.

Through all the rest of living, the disease continued its destruction. Eventually, the boys had trouble using their arms. Scoliosis set in as their back muscles atrophied; then, they lost the function of their diaphragm muscles until they could no longer breathe a sufficient amount of air to maintain life unassisted. From there on they required the use of a ventilator ~age 16. Each boy had a cardiac arrest which proceeded their chronic use of a ventilator.

Adam described having a cardiac arrest as a terrifying and traumatic event. In his view, suffocating is probably one of the worst ways to go next to being lit on fire. Willingly letting yourself go unconscious underwater is the final test for the highest tier of the elite Navy SEALs, Adam says,

"And I know there's a reason for this from personal experience."

The disease inexorably continued on its course, but the loss of muscle function stabilized at both boys retaining very limited use of their hands. Technically, they were severely quadriparetic–not quite fully quadriplegic–a distinction with little difference.

The diagnosis in early childhood is simple once signs and symptoms of the condition present themselves. The CK [Creatine Kinase] test measures the amount of CK in the blood. CK is an enzyme found in skeletal muscle, cardiac muscle, and the brain. It is released from muscle cells into the blood during muscle injury, including the progressive damage of Duchenne's.

Elevated levels almost always indicate skeletal muscle damage, can be observed as early as at birth or even in utero as in Adam's case, and are almost pathognomonic of muscular dystrophy.

Normal levels of CK are 60-305 at age 0-3 months and 75-230 at 4-6 years compared to typical elevations of 50- to 200-fold above normal levels of CK [levels >305 and 230] respectively.

Because many treatments are very specific to a particular mutation, it is common to proceed directly to **genetic testing to confirm a diagnosis of Duchenne's.** A genetic test for Duchenne's looks for a mutation in the DNA of the gene responsible for the protein dystrophin [widely known as the DMD gene] causing failure in the production of the necessary protein. There are two tests—both mouthfuls to say and difficult to remember– multiplex ligation-dependent probe amplification [MLPA, or array based]; comparative genomic hybridization [aCGH]; and next-generation sequencing [NGS].

The tests identify both large-and small-scale mutations in the DMD gene; and typically, no further genetic testing is required. These tests can identify large-scale mutations in the DMD gene, which are found in ~80% of patients. For the remaining ~20% of patients, additional genetic testing may be needed. In rare cases, genetic testing may be inconclusive. In that case, the specialist may recommend a muscle biopsy to detect the presence of dystrophin.

There is no cure for DMD at present, but therapeutic options are available that have recognizable help to slow disease progression, stabilize disease, or treat associated conditions. However, available data is insufficient to achieve scientific agreement on the numbers related to such improvement. There are basic ways to help manage the impact of the disease on the patient, including nutrition management, physical therapy, speech therapy, and/or psychosocial therapy. In Adam's case—especially to allow him to realize his potential as a writer—specialist aides had to be hired, many of whom bond with the patient for life. Those self-sacrificing aides would qualify for hero status in this book. Drug treatments are available, palliative at best.

Adam's older sister, 41-year-old Ashley Beatty, and his younger sister, 31-year-old Randi Freestone, maintain relations and contribute to Adam's care. The sisters are both likely to be carriers of the disease and would pass it on to any of their children. Ashley was confirmed to be a carrier through testing, and Randi was not tested, but she too was practically guaranteed to be a carrier. Neither sister has had a child. His mother changed her name to Kathleen Kirby when she remarried to Alan Kirby in 2010 after Arden died in 2007.

The family moved to Vernal, Utah until 1995 when Adam turned five years old. In 1995, they moved to Soldotna, Alaska. They loaded up their belongings and drove up the Alcan highway through Canada–1,387 miles long through British Columbia, Yukon, and Alaska. Some old sections of the highway were in use as local roads, while others were left to deteriorate, and still others were plowed up. They lived in a campground near the Kenai River for two weeks until they found an apartment. The family moved into a nearby house in December, 1997 and stayed there until 2010, when Adam was twenty.

He attended grade school at the Readout Elementary School, and middle school, and high school [SoHi], all in Soldotna. All three schools were within three blocks of each other. In 2020, they moved to the Hillside area outside of Anchorage. They sold that house and moved to a house in Wasilla ~40 minutes outside Anchorage. That sale took place just before the COVID-19 pandemic took hold.

Adam's disease became the obvious central point of his life, given his physical limitations and very active mind. Shortly after moving to Soldotna—~1966—the family became involved with the Muscular Dystrophy Association which helped families with family members with Muscular Dystrophy. They helped with Jerry Lewis's MDA telethon that helped raise money that funded research to find treatments for the various types of Muscular Dystrophy diseases. Adam's brother Justin was nominated as the goodwill ambassador for MDA from 1998—1999, and Adam was nominated the goodwill ambassador for 2002—2003, gaining some recognition for the disease and for the family.

In 2003, Justin was given a wish by the Make-A-Wish foundation. He chose to go to Honolulu Hawaii with the family. They visited Pearl Harbor and saw the Arizona partly in its watery grave. In 2005, it was Adam who was granted a wish, and he decided to go back to Hawaii.

~2004 Adam was prescribed prednisone to help slow the progress of his disease, but one of the side effects is that it generally weakened his bones. One day–while doing something that he had done "at least 1000 times", his femur was fractured; he developed a hairline fracture that went all the way through it, but it was a clean break. He had to wear a cast for several months while it healed, as if he needed another impediment to his physical life.

Adam chose not to be bitter about his disease and its many negative impacts on his life. Instead, he lived in his mind by reading, and for as long as he could remember, video games were a source of entertainment and offered a welcome diversion from the limitations caused by the disease, if only for a little while. His disease did not have any bearing on his ability to control a video game character, at least, not for a long time. He made the effort to spend considerable time outside and away from a screen. But– while other boys and the adults were out playing sports–he and his brother were playing extremely competitive video games against each other. Most of the time when they played against each other, and it might have seemed more like something out of a Rocky movie to the rest of the family. Over time, both boys' skills increased, and the diversion was gratifying.

Eventually, however, their disease caught up with them even with video games. Justin—the older of the two–progressively lost the ability to play any games that required a controller–basically anything that had any sort of set up like a Nintendo, they became unable to use. But, fortunately, he still had enough use of his hands to utilize a mouse; so, he could still operate a computer. But, Adam was still able to play on devices that required a controller. It was lonely not to have his partner.

Another technology that came into use at the time was the advent of online gaming. Adam was introduced and was able to compete with other players from around the country and even the world. Adam and his brother began to notice that the majority of the time Adam's playing ability far surpassed those he was competing against. He was good, really good, almost always having the top score. It was exhilarating and gratifying. He began to feel good about himself; there was something competitive at which he was a winner.

However, it did not take long for the shine to wear off the glow of winning. He and Justin learned that–a lot of the time–beating someone made the loser incredibly angry. Adam was reluctant to tell the present author about any of the things that they called him, except to say that they frequently utilized the F word. He was playing at the skill level of elite gamers that entered into the gamer equivalent of the Super Bowl which gave him a level of joy. But, for him gaming was a way beyond his obstacles; and he never wanted to go pro or big time. Games were just a form of entertainment and a way to pass the time, nothing more.

Though he was able to use a controller for video games, certain buttons were difficult for him to press. Most of the time this was not much of an issue, but it prevented him from playing certain games because they were just too difficult for him to play properly or to enjoy doing so. The desired pleasure could not be achieved on those games.

Adam is an intelligent man. He began to employ his own variations on techniques that he learned from military and SWAT team strategies which worked against other players. Those techniquesis disadvantage-avoiding strategies, gave him an extremely unique and dangerous playstyle against other players. No normal person would ever have played the way he did, because there was no reason for them to do so. His playstyle became unique enough to baffle his opponents and made him an incredibly unpredictable and successful player.

He was ruthless—just short of cheating or saying or doing anything vulgar to his opponents. He was a quintessential competitor, despite his disease-caused disadvantages. He was not just out to win; he endeavored to annihilate the opposition as efficiently and quickly as possible—to pour salt in their wounds. [Politely put]. But, as with his brother, he gradually lost the ability to play those kinds of games. Thankfully for him, both of them could use a computer by then; so, they still continued to compete against each other. They granted no quarter to each other; they tried to outsmart and out strategize each other in more intelligent video games that were closer to an extremely complicated game of chess. They enjoyed doing so right up until Justin died. It is hard to imagine a greater loss, but Adam is stoical and strong; and he bore the loss with grace as he had all the rest of what his disease foisted upon him.

Shortly after moving to Alaska, his father Arden's health began to deteriorate inexplicably and inexorably into a steady downward spiral for him. He dealt with a standard set of measures for his diabetes.But one day–out of nowhere–one of his lungs filled with fluid; and he had to be rushed to the hospital. He required a chest tube and had to stay in the hospital for several weeks before fully recovering. From that point on, things progressively got worse. He began to have trouble walking, and eventually lost the ability to walk altogether which excited fears that he, too, had muscular dystrophy. His next symptoms seemed to be like some form of ALS [Amyotrophic Lateral Sclerosis, an incurable and ultimately fatal disease]. 90 to 95 percent of ALS occurs sporadically, with no family history of the disease. His EMG [electromyogram] did not reveal ALS.

He tested negative for muscular dystrophy. Then he began having unexplainable pain which required heavy amounts of painkillers to keep under control. The pills lead to changes in his behavior, and he was not quite the same person. Then, in 2007, he died without a clear diagnosis ever being determined.

That left Adam and Justin's mother to assume full care of them, along with the boys' younger sister who still lived at home. She was not disabled and was able to provide some help. Mother Katherine was a single parent until 2010. The present author believes that Katherine qualifies for hero status, as do all the families who man-up to similar necessities.

Having caregivers in their house to take care of Justin and Adam was critical but brought its own set of challenges–primarily, the lack of privacy due to strangers being brought into their house every day of the week. Justin and Adam together, required more work than most people are prepared to deal with since they were quadriplegics who require continuous care. That led to a high turnover rate, and in almost nonstop training and retraining process for caregivers.

After losing his ability to play video games and left with the far less exciting games that were still available for him, he needed to find something else to occupy his mind and time. With a strong mind and access to electronics, Adam started writing in earnest. He taught himself how to write and published his first book, *Hyroc*, in 2019 at the age of thirty. Adam dubbed himself, "Alaskan Writer of Imaginative Creativity"; he is definitely all of that, in all senses of the tagline.

In the opinion of the present author, Hyroc is a splendid polished work of creative fantasy/science fiction because it is well written and a good story, and it is inspired by the man's disability and what it is like to deal with it. More than that, it has an inspiring message: A person who was "different" and found acceptance to be difficult, nonetheless shows the rest of the people how to make life on the planet better for everyone, largely by his example. The present author is of the confirmed belief that the main character of Hyroc is an autobiographical shadow of Adam himself, and the book is an extended metaphor of his difficult but productive life.

Hyroc is different than the boys his age. That earned him a place as an outcast and even made people fear him for no good reason. Nothing he does seems to make a difference. Still, he has been able to live a relatively normal life. But an accident shatters all this. Hunted by an enemy that will only stop with his death, he is forced to leave behind everything he has ever known. Alone and with no one to turn to for help, every day is a challenge to survive. Through his struggle he finds his way to a place where not everything he has been taught to believe is true. Inexplicable events surround him here and his past begins to be revealed.

The present author is not about to be a spoiler; read this charming and inspiring book yourself.

Adam's three books are a trilogy called *Sentinel Flame. Book 2 is--Tree of Life: A Story of Fear, Suspicion, and the Courage it takes to Overcome unimaginable Obstacles.* After surviving his encounter with a shadow demon, Hyroc now faces fear and suspicion from Elsa and Donovan. Kit hasn't been the same since the demon touched his mind, and Hyroc fears he never will be again. Things are rapidly spinning out of control, threatening to unravel his life in Elswood. The dreaded wilderness may end up becoming his only refuge, after all. But even as things become increasingly more dangerous for him, vital pieces of the puzzle of his past are revealed. He discovers strange and powerful abilities, some of which he had utilized unknowingly. He learns of his lineage, but as much as he has sought this knowledge, not all of it is what he wanted. Hyroc's life will never be the same and what does the future hold for him?

Book 3, in the series is *Outcast; When Darkness finds you, Burn it Away.*

After surviving his encounter with a shadow demon, Hyroc now faces fear and suspicion from Elsa and Donovan. Kit hasn't been the same since the demon touched his mind, and Hyroc fears he never will be again. Things are rapidly spinning out of control, threatening to unravel his life in Elswood. The dreaded wilderness may end up becoming his only refuge, after all. But even as things become increasingly more dangerous for him, vital pieces of the puzzle of his past are revealed.

He discovers strange and powerful abilities, some of which he had utilized unknowingly. He learns of his lineage, but as much as he has sought this knowledge, not all of it is what he wanted. Hyroc's life will never be the same and what does the future hold for him? Two years have passed since book 2. Hyroc is now 18 and has mastered the use of the Flame Claw. But despite his newfound powers, he is more vulnerable than ever. With the completion of his training, he is no longer protected by a Guardian, and Ursa has long since departed. Nevertheless, his unknown adversary is still out there; and Hyroc remains ignorant of the plot against him. The last two years have only heightened the suspicion and distrust that the villagers of Elswood hold toward him, and some are outright hostile.

These behaviors solely focused on him have enveloped Donovan, Elsa, and Curtis. The charity and compassion they had initially received proceeding the spider attack have all but vanished. They are outcasts, living on the razor's edge. Hyroc does what he can to help, but it's not enough. Whether or not they can remain in Elswood weighs heavily on their minds. But even as they struggle to eke out a living in the forest, darkness gathers around them.

Keller, The Ministry zealot who hunts Hyroc, has not forgotten about him and has not been idle. Quietly he has moved his pieces into position. It will take every ounce of strength for Hyroc and his friends to survive the coming storm, and everyone may not make it out of this alive.

With that cliffhanger, his and my readers are on their own to finish the books. Neither sci-fi nor fantasy nor sermons are my favorites. Of those genre, Adam's three books are by far my choices owing to my knowledge of the underlying metaphor writ large. I get the darkness and struggle, the enlightenment, and the strength of his unknown talents, and more than anything, Adam Freestone's message as told by Hyroc, his alter ego. But, his stories are never quite what they first appear to be.

"As weird as it might sound, I originally got the idea for my story from my disability. I have Duchenne muscular dystrophy, and I require a wheelchair. Due to my equipment, people treat me differently when I'm out and about. They rarely mistreat me, but it's not the same as everyone else. This is from me being in a relatively unique situation, and people don't know how to interact or react to me. And the same holds for Hyroc. He's not disabled, but he's still different than everyone else. I wondered how people might treat someone like him. And I wanted to do it for readers entertainingly and enjoyably."

–Adam Freestone

To have borne up with the hardships he has faced, the necessity to live with a good mind in a body which cannot respond, and the myriad of negative events that accompany life with DMD, one would be inclined to think of Adam Freestone as a paragon of stoicism, some saint, or a man so in control of his mind, that he can bear up with the boredom, anxiety, fear, and frustration, of his condition, with unprecedented equanimity.

There is some truth to all that, but Adam would not characterize himself that way. He is an ordinary man dealing with an extraordinary and persistent lifestyle imposed upon him. He does the best he can, better than most other people would do if they were plucked off the street and put into his life.

Anyone who knows and speaks with Adam is immediately aware of his trouble being able to speak loud enough for people to hear him and the difficult way with his struggle for his words to be understood. Adam, the Stoic, is neither unfeeling nor a Pollyanna. He readily admits that speaking is a constant source of irritation for him. The causes for the speaking difficulty stem from his ventilator breathing for him, his lack of diaphragm strength, and not being able to control his breathing. For people without Adam's disability, speech usually comes without a second thought as talking takes place during regular breathing.

Another source of frustration [and maybe a little anger] comes from the reaction of people when they see him in his wheelchair or surrounded by his medical equipment. Many people have a small shock, especially when they have likely never seen someone as disabled as he is. Disabilities of any kind arouse fear in most people, or an excess of pity, or a feeling that God must be punishing the invalid. None of those responses is helpful.

His wheelchair tends to close him off from a normal interaction, similar to what might happen if someone has their arms crossed. It basically says to that person, "I don't want to talk to anyone," which is the opposite of what he wants to happen. However, that situation only occurs when Adam first meets someone; and it goes away once they get to know him.

One of the worst causes of his frustration is that being disabled seems to cause some people to make an assumption about his mental faculties also being diminished, and that assumption seems to make them immediately write off his excellent intelligence which prevents them from fully grasping the scope of things he is saying. It is a bias towards disability in general, and towards Adam's DMD in particular. Deaf people have much the same experience; the wisdom is since they cannot hear, they cannot understand an ongoing conversation; so, they must be stupid or demented. People shout at blind people as a reflex. None of those people appreciate such isolation or treatment.

Adam is also frustrated because he has a fairly limited amount of social interaction due to his disability. It is difficult for him to go out and properly meet others. Like most young men, Adam likes to get outside and go on trails; but because of his wheelchair, oxygen tanks, etc., he is confined to fairly limited types of terrain—flat and even surface. He finds outdoors places pleasant and beautiful, but there are many places on trails where he cannot go to them because the trail is rough. A good deal of this yearning for the outdoors has to go on in his mind and in his writing. Even visiting someone's house is difficult if they have an uneven backyard. Having steps also prevents him from entering a friend's house.

There are also all kinds of frustrating and annoying things he has to deal with in order to continue getting the money he is due by law because of his disability and inability to be able to work. Strangely, the biggest issue for Adam is the fact that his cognitive abilities are unimpaired while he is physically disabled. Most of the requirements under the law are tied to mental disabilities such as autism or Down syndrome. And he does not qualify for most of the requirements, because he is not mentally disabled;

i.e. he does not fit neatly into any of the boxes the government has set up for disabled people. For example, almost every year he is required to confirm for his insurance that he remains disabled. His disability is obviously and unmistakably permanent. Nevertheless, he has to track down all kinds of paperwork, get doctors to sign off on things. Adam, the Stoic, can be forgiven if he sees that as a huge irritation and source of stress to deal with every year. It was doubly so while his brother was still living.

Among the nuisances he has to put up with includes his being very underweight. So, he was frequently prescribed supplements to try and help put on weight. When none of his doctors could figure out why; and aggravatingly, they came to think that his mother was starving him. He was eating, just not gaining any weight.

As if the family did not have enough trials to bear, in 2022, both of his sisters were diagnosed with celiac disease; and, when he was tested, Adam had it as well. It was the cause of his trouble gaining weight. Adam saw the nutritional problems as due to having stupid or ignorant doctors. He did not have an eating disorder; he had an absorption disorder.He actually became depressed by the thought that he was very intelligent; but apparently, he could not figure out how to eat properly.

> "Then, it turned out, my doctors were completely wrong. And I also think I deserved an apology from those doctors."

> -Adam Freestone

Lots of luck there.

Adam works at his writing and his life against daunting odds. Nearly all the boys he met through the MDA summer camp program in Alaska who and grew up with muscular dystrophy have died. Justin's attending physician was amazed that his brother was 38 when he died. For all his experience, he had not seen a patient with DMD live that long. Adam sees this as an accomplishment for both him and his brother since Adam is 33 now and not even near dying.

Besides his family, Adam has support he feels provides something to feel optimistic about. He is LDS [Church of Jesus Christ of Latter-day Saints]. His faith has been a big part of his life.

"Despite the terrible effects of my disability and my inability to do much of anything, it has given me something to look forward to. It comforts me that after my life is finished, I will be free of my disability and able to do all those things I couldn't. If not for this, I fear I would be incredibly depressed and furious about my situation. I don't know if I would have been able to keep my sanity if I didn't believe in that. Our faith was much more important for my brother, but he gave me an example to follow, and he was even a full Temple holder (I'm also in the midst of accomplishing this)."

Adam Freestone has accomplished major things despite his disability from the cruel disease. He taught himself how to write, and he has published three books. A great many would-be authors without disabilities never finally get even one published. Adam says,

"I don't know if I should count this as an accomplishment, but with as determined, stoic, and able to withstand hardships and discomfort, if not for my disability, I believe that I would have become a tier 1 operator or the very top echelon of Navy special forces. My father was also a freakishly good shot, and I think he would have imported that skill in me. But, this is just a nice "what if" thought."

Yes, "what if." Adam is my hero, and I have a deep wish for him that his spiritual dreams can be fulfilled.

# Heroes of World War II
## Eric Henry Liddell, 1925-1945

Eric Henry Liddell was born January 16, 1902 [in the aftermath of the Boxer rising] in Tientsin, Qing, North China to Scottish London Missionary Society missionary parents–the second son of the Reverend and Mrs. James Dunlop Liddell. He went to school in China until the age of five. At the age of six, he and his eight-year-old brother Robert were enrolled in Eltham College, a boarding school in south London for the sons of missionaries. At Eltham, Nottingham, Liddell was an outstanding athlete, earning the Blackheath Cup [Rugby union club] as the best athlete of his year. He played for the First XI and the First XV by the age of 15, later becoming captain of both the cricket and rugby union teams.

The Liddell parents and sister Jenny returned to China leaving the boys in their school. During the boys' time at Eltham, their parents, sister, and new brother Ernest, came home on furlough two or three times and were able to be together as a family, mainly living in Edinburgh.

In 1920, Liddell joined his brother Robert at the University of Edinburgh to study Pure Science. While at the university, Liddell became well known for being the fastest runner in Scotland. Newspapers carried stories of his feats at track meets, and many articles stated that he was a potential Olympic choice and probably would be a medalist. In 1923 he won the AAA Championships in athletics in the 100 and set a British record of 9.7 seconds that would not be equaled for 23 years and the 220 yards in 21.6 seconds. He opened the 1924 track season with a brief visit to America in April, where he finished second in the 200 yards and fourth in the 100 yards at the Penn Relays. He graduated with a Bachelor of Science degree after the Paris Olympiad in 1924.

Liddell was chosen to speak for the GSEU [Glasgow Student Evangelist Union] by one of the co-founders because he stood out as a committed and devout Christian. He was expected to draw large crowds to hear the Gospel. The GSEU sent out a group of eight-ten men to an area where they would stay with the local population. It was Liddell's job to be lead speaker and to evangelize the men of Scotland.

## 1924 Summer Olympics

The 1924 Summer Olympics were hosted by the city of Paris. Eric was reprimanded by his sister for neglecting his responsibilities before God as he devoted his focus toward competitive running.

Liddell responded, "I believe that God made me for a purpose. But He also made me fast, and when I run, I feel His pleasure."

Because he was a devout Christian, Liddell refused to run in a heat held on Sunday and was forced to withdraw from the 100-meters race, his best event. The schedule had been published several months earlier, and his decision was made well before the Games. Liddell spent the intervening months training for the 400 meters, though his best pre-Olympics time of 49.6 seconds–set in winning the 1924 AAA championship 440 yards— which was modest by international standards. In a classic final, Liddell— having drawn the worst position, the outside lane—he set a devastating pace–which with head back and arms flailing–he somehow managed to maintain to the crossing of the tape.

At the start of the race, Liddell went to the starting blocks, where an American Olympic Team masseur slipped a piece of paper into his hand with a quotation from 1 Samuel 2:30: "Those who honor me I will honor." The pipe band of the 51st Highland Brigade played outside the stadium for the hour before he ran. The 400 meters had been considered a middle-distance event in which runners raced round the first bend and coasted through the back leg. Inspired by the Biblical message, and deprived of a view of the other runners because he drew the outside lane, Liddell raced the whole of the first 200 meters to be well clear of the favored Americans. He came home in 47.6 seconds for a new Olympic, European, and British, record.

On July 12, 1924. E. H. Liddell–the Edinburgh University sprinter– won the 400 meters final in the world's record time of 47.35 seconds, after what was perhaps the greatest quarter-mile race ever run. With little option but to then treat the race as a complete sprint, he continued to race round the final bend. He was challenged all the way down the home straight but held on to take the win and to break the Olympic record. Harold Abrahams took Liddell's place in the sprint and won the 100 meters in a new Games record time. Abrahams' 100 meters, and Liddell's 400 meters, provided the greatest thrills of the games; and in addition, Eric Liddell broke the world record three times in two days. As significant, there was Harold Abrahams, an English Jew who ran to overcome prejudice.

Liddell's performance in the 400 meters in Paris stood as a European record for 12 years, until beaten by another British athlete, Godfrey Brown, at the Berlin Olympics in 1936. After the Olympics and graduation from Edinburgh University, Liddell continued to compete. His refusal to compete on Sunday meant he had also missed the Olympic 4 x 400 relay, in which Britain finished third. Shortly after the Games, his final leg in the 4 x 400 meters race in a British Empire vs. USA contest helped secure the victory over the gold-medal winning Americans.

Liddell ran his last race in 1930 when he won the North China Championship.

He returned to China in 1925 to serve as a missionary teacher. During his first furlough from missionary work in 1932, he was ordained a minister of religion. Aside from two furloughs in Scotland, he remained in China until his death in a Japanese civilian internment camp in 1945.

## A Hero in China:

Liddell returned to Northern China to serve as a missionary, like his parents, from 1925 to 1943; first in Tianjin and later in the town of Xiaozhang, Hengshui County. Liddell courted his future wife by taking her for lunch to the Kiesling restaurant, which is still open in Tianjin. He married Florence Jean Mackenzie—the daughter of Canadian missionaries–on March 27, 1934, in Tientsin, China [they were both 22]; and they had three daughters–Maureen, Patricia, and Heather–the last of whom he would not live to see. Maureen was still in her mother's womb when her father–Olympic runner and dedicated

Christian missionary Eric Liddell–sent his wife and two older daughters to live in Canada.

On one occasion he was asked if he ever regretted his decision to leave behind the fame and glory of athletics. Liddell responded, "It's natural for a chap to think over all that sometimes, but I'm glad I'm at the work I'm engaged in now. A fellow's life counts for far more at this than the other."

Within two years, the Japanese–fighting the Second Sino-Japanese War against the Chinese–forced Liddell into an internment camp. Two years after that, he died there. Because of his birth and death in China, some of that country's Olympic literature lists Liddell as China's first Olympic champion.

Liddell made many sacrifices in his life. He could have run on Sundays. He could have continued his career as an Olympic runner. He could have gone home with his family to safety and plenty in Canada. Instead, he gave his life to God. He did not run on Sundays. He decided that he would pursue a career as a missionary even though it meant privation and facing danger. He died in China, far away from his loved ones.

**Heroism:**

In 1925, soon after Eric graduated from Edinburgh University, he returned to China as a missionary. Liddell's first job as a missionary was as a teacher at an Anglo-Chinese College. He taught at a school in Tientsin [grades 1–12] for wealthy Chinese students. While he is best known for athletics, his true passion was found in his missionary work. It was believed that by teaching the children of the wealthy, they would become influential figures in China and promote Christian values. Liddell used his athletic experience to train boys in a number of different sports. One of his many responsibilities was that of superintendent of the Sunday school at Union Church where his father was pastor. Liddell lived at 38 Chongqing Dao [known as Cambridge Road during the British era] in Tianjin, where a plaque commemorates his former residence. He also helped build the Minyuan Stadium in Tianjin. He suggested that it be copied exactly from Chelsea's football ground, where he had competed and was said to be his favorite running venue.

In Tientsin, he fell in love with Florence MacKenzie, daughter of Canadian missionaries. He and Florence married in 1934. In 1939, Eric left the Tientsin school to work in a London Mission hospital in Siaochang, where fighting was especially intense between the Japanese and communist Chinese forces. He and his colleagues frequently risked their lives bringing aid to the wounded.

He joined his brother, Rob, who was a doctor there. The station was severely short of help and the missionaries there were exhausted. A constant stream of locals came at all hours for medical treatment. Liddell arrived at the station in time to relieve his brother, who was ill and needing to go on furlough. Florence was pregnant with their third daughter in 1941 when Eric was approached by the Japanese to be one of the very few to be allowed to leave China and to go to safety. He asked Florence to take the girls and return to Canada; and she protested against leaving without him, doubting that she would ever see him again. He insisted on staying for God and the Chinese people, and thereby squandered his last chance to live comfortably in the West. The Japanese had spread through much of China, and conditions were growing increasingly dangerous. The British government encouraged its nationals to leave; but again, Eric considered it his duty to stay behind.

As fighting between the Chinese Eighth Route Army and invading Japanese reached Xiaozhang; the Japanese took over the mission station; and Liddell returned to Tianjin.

Life in China became especially risky for Eric after that. After war was declared between Japan and the allied nations, the doors were closed; and the gates were locked. In 1943, Eric was taken by the Japanese and placed in the Weihsien Internment Camp with the members of the China Inland Mission, Chefoo School, and many others. Weihsien was a dismal place of brutality, slavery, illness, and starvation.

Living at Weihsien was one trial after another: bedbugs and rats infested the sleeping areas; there was not enough food to go around; and malnutrition, disease, and mental breakdowns, were prevalent all around him. The compound was about the size of a large city block, slightly more than 6 acres in size.

One description by an internee was, "the dilapidated compound was bare walls, bare floors, dim electric lights, no running water, primitive latrines, two houses with showers, three huge public kitchens, a desecrated church, and a dismantled hospital."

The Japanese guards lived in an adjoining area of better houses, formerly the homes of missionaries. The compound was surrounded by farmland. Eric often gave his ration to poorer Chinese internees. There were many cliques in the camp and when some rich businessmen managed to smuggle in some eggs, Liddell shamed them into sharing their eggs. While fellow missionaries formed cliques, moralized, and acted selfishly, Liddell busied himself by helping the elderly, teaching at the camp school Bible classes, arranging games and by teaching science to the children.

Despite all that, the camp's nearly 2,000 internees from thirteen different countries organized themselves commendably, partially due to Liddell's leadership and encouragement. Ultimately subordinate to the Japanese officers, they established nine committees to govern camp life. They pooled their books to create a library and held debates, lectures, and a variety of classes. One Sunday, Eric refereed a hockey match to stop fighting amongst the players, since he was trusted not to take sides.

A black market struggled along until in July, 1944 when the Japanese guards became the middlemen, facilitating the trade in exchange for a commission. The produce brought into the camp via the black marketers–whose most successful practitioners were Catholic priests and monks–was important for the nutrition of the internees. Children were given a tablespoon per day of crushed eggshells as a calcium supplement.

There were many at Weihsien besides Eric who put the needs of others before their own, Eric Liddell was arguably "one of the most popular people in the camp," for that reason. He did more than any other person for Weihsien's adolescents, survivors reported. Eric taught science from a textbook that he had reproduced from memory and organized sporting events for the children. Though doctors at other camps suggested refraining from sports to save the internees' energy, Eric operated under the belief that athletics would be beneficial, boosting the spirits of the young people.

With an infectious smile and his characteristic enthusiasm, he took on chores for the sick and elderly.

A fellow internee said of Liddell:

"Often in an evening I would see him bent over a chessboard or a model boat, or directing some sort of square dance–absorbed, weary, and interested, pouring all of himself into this effort to capture the imagination of these penned-up youths. He was overflowing with good humor and love for life, and with enthusiasm and charm. It is rare indeed that a person has the good fortune to meet a saint, but he came as close to it as anyone I have ever known."

Another Weihsien internee said of Eric: "Here was a man who was the embodiment of what the Christian faith was all about."

Despite his own dismay at being separated from his family, Eric became family to the other internees. The children knew him as "Uncle Eric." He gave the teachers from the interned Chefoo School a break one day a week when he tended their parent-less charges according to a child internee who lived to report. That reporter also noted that Eric and a roommate woke early every morning to spend one hour in the light of a peanut oil lamp studying the Bible and praying. Of Eric's relationship with Christ, the reporter wrote, "That friendship meant everything to him."

Though beginning to suffer from severe headaches, Eric continued to serve others. In February, 1945, he finally collapsed. What he mistook for exhaustion was actually a brain tumor. At his request, the camp's Salvation Army band stood outside of his hospital window and played the hymn *Be Still, My Soul*. A few days later, on February 21, Eric Liddell–aged forty-three—died in the Weifang Japanese internment camp, Putian, Fujian, China. Liddell's last words were, "It's complete surrender", in reference about how he had given his life to his God. He was buried in the garden behind the Japanese officers' quarters.

"The whole camp was in mourning, everybody loved him," an internee said.

Thirty-one people died during their internment at Weihsien, including Eric Liddell. Thirty-three children were born.

The camp's Guide and Scout companies formed an honor guard for Eric's funeral, burying him in a cemetery in the Japanese quarters. A stone was later erected on his grave.

**Legacy:**

Eric Liddell achieved fame and status as an athlete but remained humble, self-effacing, and generous. His faith in Christ translated into a practical love for those around him, leading him back to China, keeping him there despite the risk, and compelling him to serve his fellow internees cheerfully until God called him home.

"I don't need explanations from God," Eric once said. "I simply believe Him and accept whatever comes my way."

The graves in the old camp cemetery were marked only with small wooden crosses without names, but people present at the funeral recalled which was Mr. Liddell's.

A new granite stone marker for the grave has been engraved with Mr. Liddell's name, a brief biography in English and Chinese, and a quotation from *Isaiah 40 : 31 KJV:* "They shall mount up with wings as eagles; they shall run, and not be weary."

The school where Liddell taught is still in use today. One of his daughters visited Tianjin in 1991 and presented the headmaster of the school with one of the medals that Liddell had won for athletics.

In 2008, just before the Beijing Olympics, Chinese authorities revealed that Liddell had refused an opportunity to leave the camp, and instead gave his place to a pregnant woman as the two of them were in a queue to board a plane for Canada. The Japanese and British–with Churchill's approval–had agreed upon a prisoner exchange. News of this final act of sacrifice greatly impressed the ruling Chinese government and surprised even his family members.

Eric's gravesite was forgotten until it was rediscovered in 1989, in the grounds of what is now Weifeng Middle School in Shandong Province, north-east China, about six hours' drive from Beijing. Its rediscovery was largely the result of the determination of Charles Walker, an engineer working in Hong Kong, who felt one of Scotland's great heroes was in danger of being forgotten. His search for the grave proved difficult because since Liddell's death, place names had changed, documents disappeared. and witnesses were difficult to find.

On the 60th anniversary of the Weifang internment camp and Auschwitz's liberation, the United Nations General Assembly resolved the following: "With everlasting regret for the past" and "never again" resolve for the future, the United Nations today commemorated the 60th anniversary of the liberation of the Nazi death camps, symbol of the Holocaust that slaughtered at least 6 million Jews and others in World War II."

On August 17, 2005, the survivors of Weifang met at the site. Sixty-seven elderly survivors of Weixian concentration camp and their family members gathered at the former camp site in Weifang to celebrate the 60th anniversary of the camp's liberation. About 2,000 people—mainly foreigners—were put into the camp between 1942 and 1945 by the Japanese army.

The Eric Liddell Center was set up in Edinburgh in 1980 to honor Liddell's beliefs in community service while he lived and studied in Edinburgh. Local residents dedicated it to inspiring, empowering, and supporting people of all ages, cultures and abilities, as an expression of compassionate Christian values. His wife, Florence, died at age 72, on June 14th, 1984 in Hamilton, Ontario, Canada.

In 1991, Edinburgh University erected a memorial headstone, made from Isle of Mull granite and carved by a mason in Tobermory, at the former camp site in Weifang. The city of Weifang commemorated Liddell during the laying of a wreath on his grave. Eric Liddell was the most popular athlete Scotland has ever produced, according to the public voting for the first inductees for the Scottish Sports Hall of Fame in 2002.

The liturgical calendar of the Episcopal Church (USA) remembers Liddell with a feast day on February 22.

## Tuskegee Airmen, from World War I through 1941-1945

The Tuskegee Airmen as heroes represent far too many to describe their individual heroism or even to list them. The present author has selected the entirety of the group because they had to fight three wars at the same time. The first was against institutionalized American racism, segregation, inequality, and injustice—the law and social order in their home country. Those attitudes and policies carried over into the second war fought by the Tuskegee Airmen. They were initially prevented from becoming airmen, pilots, or officers. When it was clear that the war effort required the sacrifices of all Americans, the fairly new USAAF [United States Army Force] reluctantly accepted the African-American men and women who were ready and able to serve. Even then, they were commanded by frankly segregationist senior officers.

The second war to be fought by Black people was with the military—which early on did not even think their blood was worth spilling. If they were admitted to the military in any branch at all, it was for menial tasks that did not require intelligence, endurance, or patriotism. Historically, the first Blacks officially in US military service came after Abraham Lincoln's Emancipation Proclamation, January. 1, 1863. They acquitted themselves well, especially the MVIR [54th Massachusetts Volunteer Infantry Regiment]. In the post-civil war era, they served primarily in the West—most notably the 9th and 10th Cavalry and the 24th and 25th Infantry, which collectively become remembered as the "Buffalo Soldiers."

During World War I, France was lacking in adequate manpower to fight the invading German hordes. General John J. Pershing, American Expeditionary Force commander, was pressured to provide replacement troops to the exhausted French Army. Pershing decided to give the all-Black 93rd Division to the French Army. The French readily accepted the help and treated their new Black allies largely as equals. One particular regiment of the 93rd Division stood out–the 369th Infantry Regiment "Harlem Hellfighters." The 369th spent more time on the front than any other American unit and included the first Americans to be awarded the French Croix de Guerre.

After World War I, the War Department segregated blacks into all-black units; and again, they merited renown; but since the AAF [Army Air Corps] had no black units, they accepted no blacks at all. The military rejected Black men generally in the inter-war years. Despite the proven valor of Black troops, Black Soldiers represented only 1.5% of the Army in June, 1940, and roughly the same percentage of the Navy. The Marine Corps and Air Corps were off limits completely.

The Selective Training and Service Act of 1940 prohibited discrimination because of race and color and forced the War Department to accept Blacks in numerical proportion to whites. Accordingly, in 1941, the War Department forced the newly formed Army Air Forces to accept Blacks for the first time.

While some Blacks became pilots–like the well-known Tuskegee Airmen–most of these men served in support units. Although Blacks requested technical training, the AAF regularly refused their applications, as they did with Whites having low scores. All too often it appeared to Black soldiers and sailors, that they had no mission except to do menial labor and that their units served no real purpose other than providing a place to segregate Blacks.

The institutional bias toward accepting Blacks into the ranks and the professional pride exhibited by the engineers indicated that any Blacks–especially unskilled men–entering the aviation engineers faced enormous difficulties; and their performance would always be held up to unusually close scrutiny–at best. Black Americans fought in every United States conflict from the American War for Independence to present day, but they were seldom given credit or even the benefit of common decency.

The navy did not admit African-Americans until April 7, 1942. With Executive Order 9981, July 26, 1948; General Records of the United States Government; Record Group 11; National Archives, President Harry S. Truman signed the executive order banning segregation in the Armed Forces. 1948!

The third war for the Black people who had served with honor and distinction came upon their arrival back in the still segregated continental United States. Black, brown, and yellow, people served America well to establish World War II Victory. Victory at home, however, still proved elusive. Similar to Black veterans returning from World War I, the heroes of World War II often faced exclusion and aggression from the American populace.

President Harry S. Truman was especially moved by the story of Isaac Woodard. Woodard had been arrested, beaten, and blinded, by South Carolina police officers on February 12, 1946. Woodard had been honorably discharged from the Army only a few hours prior and was still in uniform when he was attacked.

President Truman took action by forming the President's Committee on Civil Rights in 1946. The committee reported to the president the pressing need to end segregation and discrimination within the Armed Forces. On July 26, 1948, Truman responded with Executive Order 9981 directing the military to end segregation. The first article stated, "There shall be equality of treatment and opportunity for all persons in the armed services without regard to race, color, religion or national origin."

Despite the order, the president faced push back from many of the leaders within the military. The leading generals argued that officers would not promote or send Black troops to schools, and that their white counterparts would become violent if forced to be together. The recent experience of combat, however, showed this to be inaccurate. The majority of men and officers who fought with Black units, reported they performed admirably and would not have issues serving alongside Black units again. White units which had not served with Black Soldiers tended to reflect the racial views the generals feared. It seemed to liberals, White intellectuals, and many decent common people who believed in the American Way, that real desegregation, equality in housing, education, the justice system, admission to hotels, motels, and restaurants, and within the military, would take an eternity to happen in any meaningful way.

The adherents to the old ingrained socially destructive life would become the parents and grandparents of the anti-vaxxers; let one example from internet e-mails suffice:

From Derek: When one studies the background of the religion of vaccination, it's hard to imagine how it became Mainstream religion it is today. The only thing that makes sense is that was done through the same means as evolution was – demonic assistance [punctuation and capitalism Derek's].

Response: "Say wha…?!"

Under the old system, the Air Force only had one Black flying group but was required to have a 10% quota of Black recruits. Regardless of how many Black Airmen were serving, they only trained enough specialists to keep the single segregated flying group in the air. Despite these men's desire to perform their trade, the majority were prohibited from doing so in the former antiquarian way. Recognizing this waste, the Air Force began adhering to the president's policy, fully integrating by 1952.

## Background of the Tuskegee Airmen:

When the Air Force began implementing its desegregation plan in 1949, future Air Force Four Star General Daniel "Chappie" James Jr.— the first Negro general in the air force–was finally sent overseas. He was fully qualified and requested to go in 1942. James was sent to Korea in July 1950 and completed 101 combat missions during his deployment. James flew 78 combat missions into North Vietnam and helped plan and lead the famed Operation Bolo in January, 1967, in what is considered the greatest air battle of that war.

Before the Tuskegee Airmen, no African-American had been a US military pilot. In 1917, African-American men had tried to become aerial observers but were rejected. The racially motivated rejections of World War I African-American recruits sparked more than two decades of advocacy by African-Americans who wished to enlist and train as military aviators. The effort was led by such prominent civil rights leaders as Walter White of the National Association for the Advancement of Colored People, labor union leader A. Philip Randolph, and Judge William H. Hastie. Finally, on April 3, 1939, Appropriations Bill Public Law 18 was passed by Congress containing an amendment by Senator Harry H. Schwartz designating funds for training African-American pilots. The War Department—not the AAF–managed to put the money into funds of civilian flight schools willing to train black Americans.

African-American Eugene Bullard served in the French air service during World War I because he was not allowed to serve in an American unit. When he was threatened to have to return to the AAF, Bullard elected to return to infantry duty with the French.

War Department tradition and policy mandated the segregation of African-Americans into separate military units staffed by white officers, as had been done previously with the 9th Cavalry, 10th Cavalry, 24th Infantry Regiment, and 25th Infantry Regiment. When the appropriation of funds for aviation training created opportunities for pilot cadets, their numbers diminished the rosters of these older units. In 1941, the War

Department and the Army Air Corps, under pressurefor three months before its transformation into the USAAF–constituted the first all-black flying unit, the 99th Pursuit Squadron.

Because of the restrictive nature of selection policies, the situation did not seem promising for African-Americans even then. In 1940, the US Census Bureau reported there were only 124 African-American pilots in the nation, let alone the military. The exclusionary policies failed dramatically when the Air Corps received an abundance of applications from men who qualified, even under the restrictive requirements. Many of the applicants had already participated in the CPTP [Civilian Pilot Training Program] unveiled in late December, 1938. Tuskegee University participated beginning in 1939. Due to the rigid system of racial segregation that prevailed in the United States during World War II, Black military pilots were trained at a separate airfield built near Tuskegee, Alabama. They became known as the "Tuskegee Airmen".

The ACTS [Air Corps Tactical School] was a military professional development school for officers of the United States Army Air Service and United States Army Air Corps–the first such school in the world. It was created in 1920 at Langley Field, Virginia and relocated to Maxwell Field, Alabama, in July, 1931. Instruction at the school was suspended in 1940, anticipating the entry of the United States into World War II; and the school was dissolved shortly after. ACTS was replaced in November, 1942 by the Army Air Force School of Applied Tactics.

In addition to the training of officers in more than 20 areas of military education, the school became the doctrine development center of the Air Corps, and a preparatory school for Air Corps officers aspiring to attendance at the US Army's Command and General Staff College. The motto of the Air Corps Tactical School was Proficimus More Irretenti ["We Make Progress Unhindered by Custom."] Little did they realize what the results would be of that motto being put into practice. Imagine the consternation that would have occurred had a Black man been admitted the prestigious training center for future generals and admirals.

For testing of applicants, the US Army Air Corps had established the Psychological Research Unit 1 at Maxwell Army Air Field, Montgomery, Alabama. Occupying the site of the first Wright Flying School, and other units around the country for aviation cadet training, the unit included the identification, selection, education, and training, ofpilots, navigators, and bombardiers. Psychologists employed in these research studies and training programs used some of the first standardized tests to quantify IQ, dexterity, and leadership qualities, to select and train the best-suited personnel for the roles of bombardier, navigator, and pilot.

The Air Corps determined that the existing programs would be used for all units, including all-black units. At Tuskegee, this effort continued with the selection and training of the Tuskegee Airmen. The War Department set up a system to accept only those with a level of flight experience or higher education which ensured that only the ablest and most intelligent African-American applicants were able to join.

Airman Coleman Young–later the first African-American mayor of Detroit–told journalist/author Studs Terkel about the process:

"They made the standards so high; we actually became an elite group. We were screened and super-screened. We were unquestionably the brightest and most physically fit young blacks in the country. We were super-better because of the irrational laws of Jim Crow. You can't bring that many intelligent young people together and train 'em as fighting men and expect them to supinely roll over when you try to f–k over 'em, right?" (Laughs).

The budding flight program at Tuskegee received a publicity boost when First Lady Eleanor Roosevelt inspected it on March 29, 1941, and flew with African-American chief civilian instructor C. Alfred "Chief" Anderson. Anderson–who had been flying since 1929 and was responsible for training thousands of rookie pilots–took his prestigious passenger on a half-hour flight in a Piper J-3 Cub. After landing, she cheerfully announced, "Well, you can fly all right."

The subsequent brouhaha over the First Lady's flight had such an impact Eleanor Roosevelt used her position as a trustee of the Julius Rosenwald Fund to arrange a loan of $175,000 to help finance the building of Moton Field. On March 22,1941, the 99th Pursuit Squadron was activated without pilots at Chanute Field in Rantoul, Illinois. A cadre of 14 black non-commissioned officers from the 24th and 25th Infantry Regiments was sent to Chanute Field to help in the administration and supervision of the trainees. A white officer, Army Captain Harold R. Maddux, was assigned as the first commander of the 99th Fighter Squadron of all Black pilots.

In June 1941, the 99th Pursuit Squadron was transferred to Tuskegee, Alabama, and remained the only black flying unit in the country but did not yet have pilots. The later-to-become–famous airmen were trained at five airfields surrounding Tuskegee University–Griel, Kennedy, Moton, Shorter, and Tuskegee, Army Air Fields. The flying unit soon consisted of 47 officers and 429 enlisted men and was backed by an entire service arm. On July 19, 1941, thirteen individuals made up the first class of aviation cadets when they entered preflight training at Tuskegee Institute. After primary training at Moton Field, they were moved to the nearby Tuskegee Army Air Field, about 10 miles to the west for conversion training onto operational types. Consequently, Tuskegee Army Air Field became the only Army installation performing three phases of pilot training [basic, advanced, and transition] at a single location. Initial planning called for 500 personnel in residence at a time. By mid-1942, over six times that many were stationed at Tuskegee, even though only two squadrons were training there.

The early group of 271 enlisted men began training in aircraft ground support trades at Chanute Field in March, 1941 until they were transferred to bases in Alabama in July, 1941. The skills being taught were so technical that setting up segregated classes was deemed impossible. This small number of enlisted men became the core of other black squadrons forming at Tuskegee Fields in Alabama. The men trained in Stearman Kaydet training aircraft, P-51s, P-51Bs, and D Mustangs. During training, Tuskegee Army Air Field was commanded first by Major James Ellison. Ellison made great progress in organizing the construction of the facilities needed for the military program at Tuskegee. However, he was transferred on January 12, 1942, because of his insistence that his African-American sentries and Military Police had police authority over local Caucasian civilians. The airmen themselves were placed under the command of Captain Benjamin O. Davis Jr., one of only two black line officers then serving.

Davis's successor, Colonel Frederick von Kimble, then oversaw operations at the Tuskegee airfield. Contrary to new Army regulations, Kimble maintained segregation on the field in deference to local customs in the state of Alabama, a policy that was deeply resented by the airmen. The new group's first commanding officer was Colonel Robert Selway, who had also commanded the 332nd Fighter Group before it deployed for combat overseas. Like his ranking officer, Major General Frank O'Driscoll Hunter from Georgia–Selway was a racial segregationist.

Hunter was blunt about it, saying such things as "...racial friction will occur if colored and white pilots are trained together."

He backed Selway's violations of Army Regulation 210–10, which forbade segregation of airbase facilities. They segregated base facilities so thoroughly that they even drew a line in the base theater and ordered separate seating by race. When the audience sat in random patterns as part of their own "Operation Checkerboard," the movie was halted to make men return to segregated seating.

African-American officers petitioned base Commanding Officer William Boyd for access to the only officer's club on base. Black Lieutenant Milton Henry entered the club and personally demanded his club rights; he was court-martialed for this—shades of Rosa Park's refusal to sit in the back of the bus. Subsequently, Colonel Boyd denied club rights to African-Americans, although General Hunter stepped in and promised a separate but equal club would be built for black airmen, something quite short of equal treatment and opportunity.

Later that year, the Air Corps replaced Kimble. His replacement had been the director of training at Tuskegee Army Airfield, Major Noel F. Parrish. Counter to the prevalent racism of the day, Parrish was fair and open-minded and petitioned Washington to allow the Tuskegee Airmen to serve in combat.

While the enlisted men were in training, five black youths—who tested as superior at the Psychological Research Unit 1–were admitted to the OTC [Officers Training School] at Chanute Field as aviation cadets. Those brilliant Black men were: Elmer D. Jones, Dudley Stevenson, and James Johnson, of Washington, DC; Nelson Brooks of Illinois, and William R. Thompson of Pittsburgh, Pennsylvania, successfully completed OTS and were commissioned as the first Black Army Air Corps Officers. And in one limited area in the United States, the walls came tumbling down.

The strict racial segregation the US Army had required gave way by practical necessity in the face of the requirements for complex training in technical vocations. The quality of the man, more than the color of his skin, required acceptance of talent when and where it was needed. Typical of the process was the development of separate African-American flight surgeons to support the operations and training of the Tuskegee Airmen. Before the development of this unit, no US Army flight surgeons had been black.

Training of African-American men as aviation medical examiners was conducted through correspondence courses, until 1943, when two black physicians were admitted to the US Army School of Aviation Medicine at Randolph Field, Texas. This was one of the earliest racially integrated courses in the US Army. Seventeen flight surgeons [medical doctors] served with the Tuskegee Airmen from 1941 to 1949. At that time, the typical tour of duty for a US Army flight surgeon was four years. Six of these physicians lived under field conditions during operations in North Africa, Sicily, and other parts of Italy. The chief flight surgeon to the Tuskegee Airmen was Vance H. Marchbanks Jr., MD, a childhood friend of Benjamin Davis.

It should come as no surprise that change did not come easily. Trained officers were also left idle as the plan to shift African-American officers into command slots stalled, and white officers not only continued to hold command but were joined by additional white officers assigned to the post. One rationale behind the active non-assignment of trained African-American officers was stated by the commanding officer of the Army Air Forces, General Henry "Hap" Arnold:

"Negro pilots cannot be used in our present Air Corps units since this would result in Negro officers serving over white enlisted men creating an impossible social situation."

The 99th was finally considered ready for combat duty by April, 1943. It shipped out of Tuskegee on April 2nd, bound for North Africa, where it would join the 33rd Fighter Group and its commander, Colonel William W. Momyer. Given little guidance from battle-experienced pilots, the 99th's first combat mission was to attack the small strategic volcanic island of Pantelleria–code name Operation Corkscrew–in the

Mediterranean Sea to clear the sea lanes for the Allied invasion of Sicily in July, 1943. The air assault on the island began May 30, 1943. The 99th flew its first combat mission on June 2. The surrender of the garrison of 11,121 Italians and 78 Germans due to air attack was the first of its kind. The 99th then moved on to Sicily and received a Distinguished Unit Citation for its performance in combat.

By the end of February, 1944, the all-black 332nd Fighter Group was sent overseas with three fighter squadrons: the 100th, 301st, and 302nd, all Tuskegee Airmen, and all Black Americans. Under the command of Colonel Davis, the squadrons were moved to mainland Italy, where the 99th Fighter Squadron, assigned to the group on May 1 1944, joined them on June 6 at Ramitelli Airfield on the Adriatic coast.

In May, 1942, the 99th Pursuit Squadron was renamed the 99th Fighter Squadron. It earned three Distinguished Unit Citations during World War II. The citations were for operations over Sicily from May 30-June 11 1943, Monastery Hill near Cassino from May 12-14, 1944, and for successfully fighting off German jet aircraft on March 24, 1945. The mission performed by the Black Tuskegee Airmen was the longest bomber escort mission of the Fifteenth Air Force throughout the entire war. The 332nd flew missions in Sicily, Anzio, Normandy, the Rhineland, the Po Valley, Rome-Arno, and others. Pilots of the 99th once set a record for destroying five enemy aircraft in under four minutes.

The Tuskegee Airmen shot down three German jets in a single day. On March 24, 1945, 43 P-51 Mustangs led by Colonel Benjamin O. Davis escorted B-17 bombers over 1,600 miles into Germany and back. The bombers' target, a massive Daimler-Benz tank factory in Berlin, was heavily defended by Luftwaffe aircraft, including propeller-driven Fw 190s, Me 163 "Komet" rocket-powered fighters, and 25 of the much more formidable Me 262s, history's first operational jet fighter. Tuskegee Airmen pilots Charles Brantley, Earl Lane, and Roscoe Brown, all shot down German jets over Berlin that day. For the mission, the 332nd Fighter Group earned a Distinguished Unit Citation.

From Ramitelli, the 332nd Fighter Group escortedFifteenth Air Force heavy strategic bombing raids into Czechoslovakia, Austria, Hungary,

Poland, and Germany. Flying escort for heavy bombers, the 332nd earned an impressive combat record. The dive-bombing and strafing missions under Lieutenant Colonel Benjamin O. Davis Jr. were highly successful.

The Allies called these airmen "Red Tails" or "Red-Tail Angels," because of the distinctive crimson unit identification marking predominantly applied on the tail section of the unit's aircraft. The red markings that distinguished the Tuskegee Airmen included red bands on the noses of P-51s as well as a red rudder; their P-51B, D Mustangs, Curtiss P-40 Warhawk, Bell P-39 Aircobra, Republic P-47 Thunderbolt, and North American P-51 Mustang fighter aircraft flew with similar color schemes, with red propeller spinners, yellow wing bands, and all-red tail surfaces.

In early April 1945, the 118th Base Unit transferred in from Godman Field; its African-American personnel held orders that specified they were base cadre, not trainees. On April 5, officers of the 477th peaceably tried to enter the whites-only officer's club. Selway had been tipped off by a phone call and had the assistant provost marshal and base billeting manager stationed at the door to refuse the 477th officers' entry. The latter–a major–ordered them to leave and took their names as a means of arresting them when they refused. It was the beginning of the so-called Freeman Field Mutiny.

In the wake of the Freeman Field Mutiny, the 616th and 619th were disbanded and the returned 99th Fighter Squadron was assigned to the 477th on June 22, 1945; it was redesignated the 477th Composite Group as a result. On July 1, 1945, Colonel Robert Selway was relieved of the Group's command; he was replaced by Colonel Benjamin O. Davis Jr. A complete sweep of Selway's white staff followed, with all vacated jobs filled by African-American officers. The war ended before the 477th Composite Group could get into action. The 99th Fighter Squadron–after its return to the United States–became part of the 477th, redesignated the 477th Composite Group.

The list of Tuskegee Airmen contains the names of military fighter and bomber pilots, airmen, navigators, bombardiers, mechanics, instructors, crew chiefs, nurses, cooks, and other support personnel who fought with honor and distinction in World War II. They were collectively awarded the Congressional Gold Medal, against all odds domestic and foreign. They were genuine heroes on all fronts of their two-front war. It is open to question whether they contributed to the long in-coming front within their home country.

## Awards:

Pilots of the 332nd Fighter Group earned 96 Distinguished Flying Crosses. Their missions took them over Italy and enemy-occupied parts of central and southern Europe.

In all, 992 pilots were trained in Tuskegee from 1941 to 1946. 355 were deployed overseas, and 84 lost their lives. The toll included 68 pilots killed in action or accidents, 12 killed in training and non-combat missions and 32 captured as prisoners of war. At the bare minimum, at least the Black Tuskegee Airmen proved beyond doubt that their blood was as valuable as that of their White comrades-in-arms.

There were 1.007 documented Tuskegee Airmen Pilots. In combat, many African American units served with distinction. The famed "Red Tails" of the 332nd Fighter Group broke down the barrier for Black pilots and air crews. Products of the segregated Tuskegee Army Airfield the 332nd flew more than 15,000 sorties, destroyed 261 enemy aircraft, and was awarded more than 850 medals.

Benjamin O. Davis, Jr., graduate of the first class of Tuskegee Airmen and commander of the 332nd went on to form the 477th Bomber Squadron, but only after many Civil Rights leaders commented on the fact that Black pilots were not allowed to fly larger aircraft like bombers.

During the service of the Black Tuskegee Airmen, a remarkable set of accomplishments was recorded:

- 1578 combat missions, 1267 for the Twelfth Air Force; 311 for the Fifteenth Air Force
- 179 bomber escort missions, with a good record of protection, losing bombers on only seven missions and a total of only 27, compared to an average of 46 among other 15th
- Air Force P-51 groups—almost all, nearly entirely manned by White personnel
- 112 enemy aircraft were destroyed in the air, another 150 on the ground, and 148 damaged. This included three Messerschmitt Me 262 jet fighters shot down

- 950 rail cars, trucks and other motor vehicles were destroyed
- One torpedo boat was put out of action.
- 40 boats and barges were destroyed.

Awards and decorations:

Three Distinguished Unit Citations:

- 99th Pursuit Squadron: May 30-June 11, 1943, for actions over Sicily
- 99th Fighter Squadron: May 12-14, 1944: for successful airstrikes against Monte Cassino, Italy. The first two Distinguished Unit Citations received by the 99th Fighter Squadron were awarded to the groups to which the squadron was attached. At the time, when a group received the honor, it was shared with the squadrons that were assigned or attached to the group
- 332nd Fighter Group [and its 99th, 100th, and 301st Fighter Squadrons]: March 24, 1945: for a bomber escort mission to Berlin, during which pilots of the 100th FS shot down three enemy Me 262 jets. The 302nd Fighter Squadron did not receive this award since it had been disbanded on March 6, 1945
- At least one Silver Star
- 96 Distinguished Flying Crosses to 95 Airmen; Captain William A. Campbell was awarded two.
- 14 Bronze Stars
- 744 Air Medals
- At least 60 Purple Hearts

More than a Band of Brothers, the Tuskegee Airmen were a Band of Heroes.

## The Six Triple Eight 1945

**Background:**

The news covered the remarkable exploits of the allied forces as they swept across former Nazi territory in Europe at a running pace. The news was about great battles, ruined cities, armies, liberated cities and countries, and the joys at home for the seemingly endless season of victory. There was very little said about the soldiers, sailors, and airmen, who were shedding their blood and lives for the enterprise. Their families wrote letters by the thousands to buoy up the spirits of their loved ones locked in the fast-moving battle, but the mail was not going anywhere. Because the war was moving too rapidly to get mail to a certain address, mail piled up hour-by-hour and day-by-day inside warehouses in Birmingham, England. Soon, boxes of letters were stacked to the rafters, and thousands more came pouring in every day.

Another problem for getting the mail to its intended man or woman in the thick of the battles was that there were not enough qualified postal officers or workers to receive, sort, and send, the missives with any degree of efficiency or accuracy. So, the letters sat in warehouses and accumulated. The problem was massive, like nothing else in history. More than seven million American servicemembers serving in the theater were constantly on the move and the sheer and ever-increasing volume of mail created a colossal logjam.

As in many such problems facing the allied advance, the solution came in the form of heroes. In this case, the heroes were the members of the 6888th Central Postal Directory Battalion which arrived on the scene in February, 1945 under the command of Major Charity Adams. On the way over to England, they were chased by a submarine and had to engage in a shootout.In a stopover in Glasgow, a German VI rocked exploded sending the battalion to seek cover. The first unique aspect of the battalion was that all the members were African-women, including the commanding officer. The second unique aspect was that they set to work with an unimaginable determination, efficiency, and will to work. Together, they sorted mail in cold, dim warehouses where rats nibbled at packages of rotted fruit. The women stayed warm by wearing long johns and extra layers of clothing. They got the herculean job done.

The African-American women knew they were under nearly constant watch. When a general demanded to know why some members of the battalion were not present for an inspection, Maj. Adams tried to explain that some were working their shifts and others were sleeping to be ready for their next shift. The general told her that he would send a white male lieutenant to show her how to lead her unit.

She risked censure, even court marshal by replying, "Over my dead body."

Later, that same general had to announce official praise for the 6888's work.

The soldiers of the 6888th were patriotic Americans who recognized the value of their war effort in raising the morale of the individual intended GIs and of the value to the overall war effort as well. They might have been angry, resentful women as a result of the maltreatment they received from their fellow citizens. They might have been lazy and nonchalant by treating their work as just another job. They were women, and they were Black; and they were not famous, important, or newsmakers. But, they were heroes, one and all. They set aside any grievances they might have had; they ignored the racism and sexism that dominated their world back home and set about their tasks with a will that was indefatigable and enormously and satisfyingly successful.

First, they studied what had to be done. They developed a card file to follow individual servicemembers, used serial service numbers to trace the many GIs with the same name—as many as 7500 Robert Smiths. In short order, they were processing 65,000 pieces of mail *per shift*, three eight hour shifts a day. They found both a will and a way to deal with the many wrong addresses, the "undeliverables", and were even able to send return letters and packages to the states. They paid special attention to getting packages to the families of the fallen.

The 6888 was the first and only African-American WAC [Women's Army Corps] deployed overseas in World War II. By the miracle of endeavor, exhaustingly hard work, and emulative efficiency, the 6888's women removed the postal backlog in three months. The military had estimated a period of six months at the very least. After they cleared the backlog in England, they were sent on to Rouen, France to tackle another massive pile. Again, they did their work in half the allotted time.

"They did their job with dignity and dedication, even though they were faced daily with prejudices… They didn't ask for pity. They had volunteered to come into the Army and serve their country when their country really did not serve them, knowing that when they got out, they would go back to a country that discriminated against them because of their race. They didn't get a parade. They didn't get an award. There was no 'thank you for your service.' But it did not despair them."

–Elizabeth HelmFrazier, Army master sergeant, Ret.

Three out of the four women buried in the Normandy American Cemetery were from the 6888th. Unit members pooled their money to pay for their caskets. At the end of their service, the women of the Six-Triple-Eight, bought their own tickets home to the United States and talked little about what they had seen and done. To a woman, they remained satisfied with their work, however.

Seventy-five years later, and too late for many of them, the 6888 received the attention they had so long deserved. A documentary and the US Senate unanimously awarded them the Congressional Gold Medal for the battalion. In 2018, five of the living members were interviewed for national recognition at the time of the dedication of a memorial to their battalion at the Buffalo Soldier Monument Park in Fort Leavenworth, Kansas.

Nearly 6,500 African-American women served on active duty during World War II. Of that number 855 women [31 officers and 424 enlisted] made up the 6888th.

"They were trailbrazers. I call them 'pioneer patriots'. They put patriotism above everything else and saw military service as an opportunity to contribute to the war effort… They were the best of the best. Others had tried and failed to clear that backlog. They were not expected to achieve, and they overachieved."

–Edna Cummings, Army Colonel, Ret.

"Beyond that, the women of today stand on the 6888's shoulders. They paved the way. You've got women going into the infantry, into the field artillery, and through Ranger School all because the Six Triple Eight laid the foundation."

–Elizabeth HelmFrazier, Army master sergeant, Ret.

## Edward Geary Lansdale

### [b. February 6, 1908 in Detroit, Michigan, d. February 23, 1987, at age 79, in McLean, Virginia]:

Major General Lansdale is a genuine military, diplomatic, and espionage agent, hero; and only a few Americans are aware of the man's importance to the country. The present author will present his history in divided segments in order to do him justice and to inform the readers of Gen. Lansdale's actions and to keep them straight during the several crises our country faced in a narrow historical period.

Lansdale was born in Detroit, Michigan, on February 6, 1908–and later reared in Los Angeles–the second of four sons of Sarah Frances Philips and Henry Lansdale. Lansdale grew up as a typical American boy of his time. He was a Boy Scout, had a paper route, worked on a bread route, fought and played with his brothers. He sold the Saturday Evening Post on street corners and made a B average in school. Lansdale attended school in Michigan, New York, and California.

After graduating from high school in 1926, Lansdale enrolled in UCLA [University of California at Los Angeles] where he earned his way largely by writing for newspapers and magazines. In 1931, he left UCLA with a bachelor's degree and a second lieutenant of infantry ranking in the US military reserves. He later moved on to better-paying work in advertising in Los Angeles and San Francisco. He started a family with Helen Batcheller. They married in 1933 and eventually had two children. She died in 1972, and Lansdale married Patrocinio Yapcinco a year later. There was nothing particularly remarkable about the young man, let alone anything world changing.

Had it not been for the United States entering the Second World War, we would likely never have heard of Edward Lansdale. His life and career were summed up by his old spy master:

"[Lansdale was] one of the greatest spies in history. [His] accomplishments were the stuff of legends."

–Former CIA Director William Colby.

# World War II

When the United States became involved in World War II in 1941, Lansdale immediately applied to return to active military service. But when action on his application was delayed, he began to look for other ways to serve his country during the war. In 1942, he used political and military contacts to gain acceptance into the OSS [US Office of Strategic Services— an agency whose responsibilities including responsibility for espionage and for helping the resistance movement in Europe, including intelligence-gathering and secret spy missions against America's enemies]. In 1947, this agency became the CIA [Central Intelligence Agency].

In February, 1943, Lansdale's request for a return to active service was finally granted. The Army made him a first lieutenant and assigned him to its Military Intelligence Service for "limited service." But as the war progressed, Lansdale spent most of his time working for the OSS. After several wartime promotions, he was transferred to Headquarters Air Forces Western Pacific as a major in 1945, where he became chief of the Intelligence Division. He transferred to the US Air Force in 1947–after it became an independent branch of the US armed force–and was ultimately promoted to major. He extended his military tour to remain in the Philippines until 1948, but he remained closely associated with the CIA.

According to biographer Sterling Seagrave, Lansdale was sent by General Charles Willoughby to the Philippines after the war. Lansdale immediately "joined the torture sessions of Japanese Major Kojima Kashii as an observer and participant". As Seagrave explained: "Since Yamashita had arrived from Manchuria in October, 1944 to take over the defense of the Philippines, Kojima had driven him everywhere."

In charge of Kojima's torture was an intelligence officer named Severino Garcia Diaz Santa "Santy" Romana. He wanted Major Kojima

Carl Douglass

to reveal each place to which he had taken General Tomoyuki Yamashita, where bullion and other treasure were hidden. Some witnesses argued that between 1945 and 1947 the gold bullion recovered by Santy and Lansdale was moved by ship to 176 accounts at banks in 42 countries. Robert Anderson and CIA agent Paul Helliwell set up these black gold accounts to provide money for political action funds throughout the noncommunist world.

After being promoted to the rank of major, Lansdale was appointed Chief of the Intelligence Division in the Philippines. His main task was to rebuild the country's security services.

## The Philippines

Lansdale extended his military tour of duty to remain in the Philippines until 1948, helping the Philippine Army rebuild its intelligence services and resolve the cases of large numbers of prisoners of war. According to Sterling Seagrave's history, Lansdale "was in and out of Tokyo on secret missions with a hand-picked team of Filipino assassins, assassinating leftists, liberals, and progressives."

In World War II, he served with the Office of Strategic Services and later was commissioned as a lieutenant in the US Army in 1943, serving in various military intelligence assignments throughout the war. During this period, he helped the Philippine Army rebuild its intelligence services, was responsible for the disposition of unresolved cases of large numbers of prisoners of war involving many nationalities, conducted numerous studies to assist the U.S. and Philippines Governments in learning the effects of World War II on the Philippines, and later served as public information officer for PHILRYCOM.

On his return to the United States in 1948, Lansdale became a lecturer at the Strategic Intelligence School at Lowry Air Force Base, Colorado, where he received a temporary promotion to lieutenant colonel in 1949. However, in 1950, Elpidio Quirino, the president of the Philippines, requested Lansdale's help in his fight against the communist insurrection taking place in his country. Quirino asked that Lansdale be transferred to the PHILRYCOM [Far East Command, United States], which became the AFWESPAC [Army Forces, Western Pacific, Philippines], and the CIA complied.

The CIA was willing to give Lansdale–a San Francisco advertising executive before World War II–great latitude based on his success in black operations in the Philippines from 1950-53. Lansdale was made liaison officer to Secretary Magsaysay for JUSMAG [Joint United. States Military. Assistance Group]. The two became intimate friends, frequently visiting the combat areas together. Lansdale helped the Philippine Armed Forces develop psychological operations, civic actions, and the rehabilitation of Huk prisoners in projects such as EDCOR. He was given a temporary promotion to colonel in 1951. Lansdale became friends with Ramon Magsaysay—who was minister of national defense at the time–and with his help Magsaysay eventually became President of the Philippines on December 30, 1953. Lansdale ran Magsaysay's campaign for the CIA in the 1953 Philippines General Election. Lansdale helped the Philippine Armed Forces develop psychological operations, civic actions, and the rehabilitation of Hukbalahap prisoners.

In the early 1950s, CIA Director Allen Dulles gave Lansdale $5-million to finance CIA operations against the Hukbalahap movement–the rural peasant farmers fighting for land-reform in the Philippines.

The Hukbong Bayan Laban sa Hapon/ Hukbalahap [People's Army Against Japan], was a Filipino communist guerrilla movement formed by the farmers of Central Luzon in 1942. They were originally formed to fight the Japanese, but extended their fight into a rebellion against the Philippine government, known as the Hukbalahap Rebellion, in 1946. The Huks—as they were popularly known—and their rebellion was finally put down through a series of reforms and military victories by Defense Secretary, and later President, Ramon Magsaysay.

After Huk efforts to participate in the postwar government were rebuffed and a reportedly fraudulent election took place in 1949, the Huks began their guerrilla war to overthrow the US backed government. In waging war against the Huks, Lansdale wielded a wide array of counterinsurgency and psywar tools, some playing upon Filipino superstitions. One such successful unconventional tactic exploited villagers' belief in vampires, another on ghosts of dead Huks. In Lansdale's "Eye of God" campaign, suspected guerrillas living in a village were targets of psywar teams that surreptitiously painted a menacing eye on a wall facing the suspect's hut.

The US-Philippine government campaign against the Huks from 1946-1954 offers important insights into limited US intervention on behalf of a foreign government. The Huk campaign may provide important lessons for future interventions and serve as a critical comparison for operations in Iraq and Afghanistan going forward. In adopting a strategy requiring popular support, the US clearly needed a strong Filipino counterpart. However, this person could not be a puppet or merely an expedient tool. The severity of the situation by 1950 required an individual capable of both winning popular support away from the Huks–a movement that already enjoyed widespread support–while surviving attacks from the entrenched, elite establishment. Edward Lansdale was the right person in the right place at the right time.

Ramon Magsaysay and Edward Lansdale successfully executed a counterinsurgency campaign against the Huk movement because of their shared empathy, deep sociocultural understanding of the Filipino people, and their complimentary capabilities and resources. The evidence clearly suggests that Magsaysay's programs and initiatives, and Lansdale's covert operations, demonstrated their empathy and sociocultural understanding, but would have been impossible without their complimentary capabilities and resources.

After Huk efforts to participate in the postwar government were rebuffed and a reportedly fraudulent election took place in 1949, the Huks began their guerrilla war to overthrow the U.S.-backed government. In waging war against the Huks, Lansdale wielded a wide array of counterinsurgency and psywar tools, some playing upon Filipino superstitions. Lansdale was an early practitioner—a pioneer–of psychological warfare. Adopting a tactic previously used in the Philippines by the Imperial Japanese Army during World War II, Lansdale spread rumors that Aswangs–blood-sucking demons in Philippine folklore–were loose in the jungle. His men then captured an enemy soldier and drained the blood from his body, leaving the corpse where it could be seen and making the Hukbalahap flee the region.

Another such successful unconventional tactic exploited villagers' belief in vampires, another in ghosts of dead Huks. In Lansdale's "Eye of God" campaign, suspected guerrillas living in a village were targets of psywar teams that surreptitiously painted a menacing eye on a wall facing the suspect's hut. Although most notorious for these types of psywar operations, it was primarily Lansdale's application of advertising principles and media manipulation that led to the honest election of Ramon Magsaysay as president in 1954.

Lansdale became friends with Ramon *Magsaysay,* then the secretary of national defense, and with his help, *Magsaysay* eventually became President of the Philippines. Their combined focus on the role that empathy and sociocultural understanding played in defeating the Huks and restoring the Philippine government's legitimacy.

Until that time, US policy in the Philippines had bolstered regimes riddled with corruption, graft, and nepotism, reinforcing poor governance and resulting in a loss of government legitimacy in the minds of the Philippine people. That heavy handed error energized the Huk movement until they were on the verge of toppling the current government. Magsaysay and Lansdale and a change in US attitude towards the value of corrupt leaders, reversed the Huks momentum, rejuvenated the demoralized and oppressed armed forces, and restored the Philippine governments legitimacy and its popular support, all in less than four years.

During that post war era, American interest in counterinsurgency apparently emerged only when confronted by insurgency, and American policy bounced from crisis to crisis. The US military focused on the conventional Soviet threat–the so-called "Domino Effect" rather than lessons learned by the soldiers and officers on the ground from irregular conflicts. That includes the counterinsurgencies in Vietnam, Afghanistan, and Iraq, and other examples of small-scale counterinsurgency campaigns. By contrast, US assistance to the Philippine government against the Huks—from 1946-1954–provides an excellent case study of limited, yet successful, intervention.

Philippine society–particularly those areas most affected by the Huk rebellion–existed under a paternalistic system whereby the landlords and elites acted as the benefactors or protectors of their patrons and the lower classes, which—in turn—remained dependent and weak. The Philippine and US governments were combatting an enemy whose main propaganda messages resonated with a popular base that had grown further and further from the landlord and elite class even before the Japanese invaded in 1941. The effects of the horrendous war and Japanese occupation exacerbated and accelerated the divide. The first and most important things for the US and Philippine leaders was to gain an accurate insight for the lower classes plight and understanding of the ills plaguing the islands' society.

In fact, forty years of US colonial rule over the Philippines left American officials with an abundance of institutional knowledge of pre-war Philippine society and culture, and that led to 180° wrong choices because no one paid attention. In the immediate post-war period, the US and Philippine governments adopted policies that failed to acknowledge societal dislocation brought on by the war and in most cases worked to counter potentially beneficial status quo changes actively. Instead, it reinforced a return to the status quo ante, and a return to power of the same men the Huks fought against during the occupation.

The war had decimated the Philippine economy. A pre-independence assessment by United States Army Forces Western Pacific intelligence staff painted a discouraging picture, stating that it "was far worse than what was envisioned in 1941," and went on to provide a worrisome summary:

"Property damage alone is estimated between $700 and $800 million. The Philippine government faces probable expenditures of ⊠186 million for its first fiscal year, with an estimated income of only ⊠6 million... Foreign trade is too scant to sustain the Philippine economy as formerly. The cost of living has risen to 6-1/2 times the pre-war level, while the 1945-46 food crop is 30% below normal. Many necessities of life are nearly impossible to obtain except through the black market... in Manila alone, there was 70% damage to housing... Nearly 80% of the schools need to be rebuilt. Only 40% of the pre-war power plants are operating today. In this uphill economic battle another significant issue hindered the Philippines, the structure of the Philippine economy under U.S. sovereignty."

Another factor contributing to the growing failure of the Philippines as a nation was the previous colonial attitude towards third-world countries as sources to be exploited. As US business interests found a ready market for consumer goods in the Philippines—as well as an abundant source of raw materials and commodities–the local economy developed to meet the demand. The development was unbalanced at best. US interests focused on raw material and commodity extraction rather than developing locally based industry and manufacturing. Indigenously manufactured consumer goods were unnecessary in the Philippines because US goods were readily available for import and relatively cheap. The economic imbalance fostered dependence and was incentivized by an absence of tariffs between the Philippines and the United States.

Thus–for the Huks and their supporters–independence signaled a continuation of the struggle against a government that looked strikingly similar to the collaborationist government.

Unfortunately, senior US officials in Manila were either holdovers from the prewar US High Commission in the Philippines, or were imported from elsewhere in Asia—especially– recruited from all the old China hands and all old Philippine colonial hands who had learned nothing useful during their indolent, self-interested country club life-styles maintained in secure and isolated compounds.

Most of the landlords and elites who could have represented the leadership of Central Luzon fled to the cities and collaborated with Japanese occupation forces. Pre-war peasant and labor leaders stepped into the void, raising local guerrilla groups, easily coalescing into the Hukbalahap guerrillas in March, 1942. The Huks remained autonomous from the US directed guerrilla groups in the Philippines. The American government and military failed to see the value of cooperation with the mass of Philippine people which frequently brought the two entities into conflict. That resulted in an inadequate force against the sadistic Japanese, fostered a sense of American abandonment during the occupation, and the Huks gaining steadily increasing control over the region.

The US counterinsurgency effort in the Philippines necessitated a significant degree of trust, a concept that had to wait for Edward Lansdale and Ramon Magsaysay to come together in a fruitful union. Trust on the part of officials in Washington for their personnel in the Philippines, and trust on the part of the masses in their own officials and government had to be achieved or the Philippines were going to be lost to the Communist hegemony and juggernaut. The former could be given; the latter had to be earned, yet both required individuals worthy of that trust. Lansdale and Magsaysay both focused on the importance of their shared empathy for the Filipino people, sociocultural understanding, and complimentary capabilities and resources; and that proved to be key.

In the early 1950s, Allen Dulles gave Lansdale $5-million to finance CIA operations against the Hukbalahap movement, the rural peasant farmers fighting for land-reform in the Philippines—a good first move in the right direction.

The origins of the two government's problems in handling the Huks stemmed from the war and its immediate aftermath. In the case of the Philippine government, the problem lay in their changing society and the development of Philippine democracy. Though class and social divisions existed long before the emergence of the Huk movement, by 1946 these divisions had grown to a point where conflict was almost unavoidable. Exacerbating this division was a political system that favored the few while failing to represent the many. The status quo may have remained for some time; but the outbreak of war in 1941; and the Filipino experience under Japanese occupation, brought the long simmering conflict to a head.

The Philippines represented the center piece of US post-war decolonization policy in the region. America could not be seen to be interfering in Philippine domestic matters. Underpinning all these issues—and informing all US actions in the Philippines at the time—was the threat of communism. The war and occupation led to the evolution of the Huk insurgency from a localized problem to a national crisis. Those Filipinos who collaborated with the Japanese—particularly the elite and land-owning class—served as a focal point for Huk and peasant animosity and retaliation during the Japanese occupation, unleashing a cycle of post-war violence that would come close to toppling the Philippine government. The US government took the myopic view held by Senator Joseph McCarthy and the House Unamerican Activities Committee. "There is a world-wide Communist threat... If your mommy is a commie, you have to turn her in."

The Hukbalahap [*Hukbong Bayan Laban sa mga Hapon* or People's AntiJapanese Army] was an armed resistance movement established by the United Front on March 29, 1942. The Huk would grow to become one of the largest and most powerful guerrilla organizations in central Luzon. The PKP [The Philippine Communist Party–*Partido Komunistang Pilipina* or PKP] of the 1930s was a fairly weak organization with a small support base, having been outlawed by the Commonwealth government, and lacking a narrative that resonated with the average Filipino. It exercised varying degrees of control over the local leadership of the organization during the occupation–largely because so many of the senior Huk leaders were also leaders within the PKP–but the rank-and-file consisted of peasants with little to no communist indoctrination.

The Hukbalahap rank-and-file consisted of peasants with little to no communist indoctrination, at least early on. Western power policy altered that statistic in a negative way for the US. In 1942, their supreme military commander Luis Taruc, sent a letter to General MacArthur pledging allegiance to both the US and Philippine governments, and requesting guidance and support, neither of which was forthcoming, which turned out to be a deadly mistake.

The Huks decided to maintain autonomy from other US-led guerrilla units and initiated an aggressive campaign against Japanese forces and the collaborationist government on its own. The Huks are alleged to have killed 25,000 people in the Philippines during the occupation; of that number only 5,000 were Japanese. And still the US and US dominated Philippine governments ignored the obvious. The governments and their intelligence agencies saw those statistic as a reign of terror throughout Central Luzon and as another reason for the US government not to recognize the Huks formally as pro-Philippine guerrillas after the war.

Luis Taruc admitted that there were elements within the movement that engaged in unacceptable behavior, such as theft and murder; but even the American leadership of the United States Army guerrilla units acknowledged that their own Filipino personnel used the chaos of the occupation to settle old scores and rivalries with atrocities. Attempts to collaborate failed almost every time. On numerous occasions the two sides attempted meetings that were either broken up or ambushed by Japanese and collaborationist PC forces.

The US military and fledgling Philippine Army were defeated by the Japanese. The new rulers and their allies in the collaborationist government quickly set to work, attacking the Huks and their support base. The poorly trained, equipped, and led, collaborationist constabulary forces resorted to brutality to compensate for their deficiencies. The lawlessness of the period–combined with Japanese support for the elites– meant there were few limitations to the depredations in Central Luzon during the occupation.

By a huge miscalculation, the man General MacArthur relied on the most to lay the groundwork for post-liberation Philippine policy firmly believed in a return to the status quo ante which resulted in chaos, stagnation, and corruption. The almost willful ignorance of US officials regarding the growing social conflict in the immediate post-war period contributed to almost five years of ill-informed Philippine policy until Lansdale and Magsaysay united to reverse directions.

Ho Chi Minh's Viet Minh forces in Indochina had already declared a republic and initiated hostilities toward Chinese nationalist and Indian Army forces by the time the French returned after the war. Meanwhile, Filipino nationalist sentiment was strong and growing. Following the Japanese surrender in September 1945, 50,000 U.S. troops remained in the Philippines to take part in this "no fail" mission. This number rapidly decreased as the US downsized its military forces generally and was forced to commit troops to occupation duties in Europe and elsewhere in Asia at the expense of the Philippine public.

Reconstruction and rehabilitation of the Philippines lagged far behind what should have been accomplished given the hundreds of millions of dollars in aid provided by the US government. The ambassador to the Philippines at the time recalled: "Events elsewhere in the world distracted officials in Washington from the developing crisis in the Philippines... I had been called by Dean Acheson and told that, 'I've got a lot of things to do, a lot of things on my mind. You're on the Philippine desk now. You go ahead and decide what has to be done,'" and summarily ignored the loyal people of the Philippines.

US policy was inadvertently supporting a Philippine government trend towards authoritarianism which was undermining popular government legitimacy. The massively corrupt 1949 general elections gave the incumbent Elpidio Quirino another four years at the helm of a country without a rudder. Quirino lacked integrity, and was both physically, ethically, and morally weak. By June, 1950, Central Intelligence Agency analysts predicted Quirino's imminent down-fall, noting that "despite an oppressive disregard for civil rights, [he] has been unable to maintain law and order, and has permitted excessive graft, corruption, and inefficiency."

Industry was largely ignored. The public works sector deteriorated so badly that teachers went without pay for up to three to four months. Despite large expenditures for residential construction in the Philippines–particularly in Manila–there was virtually no change in living conditions for the lower classes suggesting that most of the funds, including public funds from taxes, went towards construction in only upper class areas. Despite the windfall profits of the wealthy, the tax burden remained largely on the lower classes, all of which caused the Philippine government to face a crisis of legitimacy.

By the close of 1949, the Philippine government had squandered hundreds of millions of dollars, with US consent and US citizen' tax dollars. They rebuilt a pre-war economy not suited to economic independence into one even worse. Elpidio Quirino secured the presidency aided by millions of pesos donated grudgingly by Chinese businessmen under pressure from the KMT-controlled Chinese chambers of commerce in Manila. The 1949 election reinvigorated the Huk movement by providing them with a popular and undeniable narrative about the government's irretrievable state.

Edward Lansdale truly represented a practical case of the right person, in the right place, at the right time. Lansdale's personality and professional development prepared him for the challenges he faced in the Philippines. His personality played an important part in his actions in his new assignment. He possessed deep convictions about the importance of his work in fighting communism, but more importantly in promoting democracy and democratic ideals. Lansdale's journal–from his early days in the Philippines–demonstrates that he genuinely cared about the plight of the lower classes, particularly those in the provinces, applying blame equally to the Huks and the corrupt PC [Philippine Constabulary] for the peasants' suffering.

In describing Lansdale, Ramon Magsaysay's son noted that:

"he was nice. He was not rough or tough. He [had] good rapport with ordinary people. I think that's why my father got close to him, because they were both sensitive of ordinary people… He was sincere. He didn't ruffle feathers. He was quiet . . . he was more observing." All of these characteristics contributed to a charisma that naturally attracted people to him, and allowed him to work with individuals from diverse backgrounds."

His work with the OSS exposed him to the usefulness of clandestine activities; Lansdale professed the belief that the United States should not simply be anti-communist, but they must put forth a positive program that built optimism and hope. The OSS also broadened his horizons in terms of who might prove useful in intelligence work. Working with the OSS in the Pacific Theater also provided him a geographic orientation that would remain for the vast majority of his career.

Following the war–with his unconventional OSS days behind him–Lansdale was assigned to the conventional G-2 [Intelligence] section of US Army Forces Western Pacific–based in the Philippines–from 1945-1948.

Prior to an anti-Huk PC operation Lansdale looked at maps of the intended operations area and identified likely Huk escape routes. He then drove a jeep to one of the identified routes and after encountering a Huk unit, spent time talking to them, sharing beer and cigarettes. Such missions helped shape his understanding of the Huks as individuals. The Huks were no longer faceless, dogmatic communists to Lansdale, but individuals with unique and perhaps justifiable motivations for fighting the government.

Lansdale's rapidly increasing appreciation of the problems in the Philippines yielded a later observation that "90% of the officers hadn't the least idea of what was going on for the Wack Wack [Country Club] is still operating; and there are lots of dependents living here now; and the Army has started drawing off into its own little community." Ambassador Cowen identified a similar problem within the diplomatic corps.

Major Lansdale was given the task of rebuilding the American military's image in the Philippines through the Public Information Office. This position was to prove extremely important in Lansdale's development since he insisted upon core genuine improvements. Lansdale developed a substantial social network that included businessmen, industrialists, and local, provincial, and national, level government officials. Combined with his provincial trips that allowed him to meet with the lower classes, Lansdale's network encompassed virtually all social classes.

When Lansdale left the Philippines with his family in 1948, more than a hundred Filipinos came to see them off. He left his mark on the hearts of his Filipino friends during his first assignment, but it would take his next assignment in the Philippines for him to leave his mark on the country's history.

Congressman Ramon Magsaysay was building a name for himself not only in his home province of Zambales, but on the national scene as well. Magsaysay spent his early years in Zambales as the son of a trade school teacher, in a simple house. Despite the myth cultivated about his supposedly humble background, he in fact came from a family that owned several farms–one in excess of 1,000 acres–and a general store.

In 1940, as branch manager of a bus company, Magsaysay broke a strike that was itself called in protest at his high-handed disciplinary methods.

An early life lesson impressed on Magsaysay the cost of adhering to principles and ideals. His teacher father failed the son of the trade school's superintendent and was fired. Despite the family's crisis, Ramon Magsaysay took the lesson to heart and continued to learn from his very principled father. Magsaysay started working at the age of seven and continued to work throughout his childhood in order to help make ends meet for his family. During this period, he began working in his father's small blacksmith shop where he developed a lifelong interest in all things mechanical, and which started him down a road that would lead to the presidency.

Magsaysay became a mechanic for the Try Tran bus company in 1931. Working for Try Tran brought him intervals of relative prosperity and absolute misery. Fortunes of the company rose and fell; so, Ramon and his newly formed family learned what it was to live in poverty. When the Japanese invaded the Philippines in late 1941, the Try Tran company was commandeered by the US military to transport soldiers. Magsaysay volunteered his services and because of his skills was commissioned as a captain in the 31st Division's motor pool, under the command of Colonel Napoleon Valeriano.

When Bataan fell, Magsaysay and his unit were still in Zambales. Rather than surrender, they organized themselves into a guerrilla unit under the command of Colonel Gyles Merrill, Col. guerrilla commander on West Luzón. As an officer in the Zambales Guerrillas or Merrill's Marauders–as they came to be known–Magsaysay excelled at motivating his fellow Filipino guerrillas, but held one belief that caused him grief with both his countrymen and the Americans. He believed in reconciliation with collaborators. Rather than executing or assassinating collaborators, Magsaysay argued on their behalf.

Presidential candidate Manuel Roxas invited him to Manila and offered him a seat on his ticket for the upcoming election in 1946. Magsaysay turned him down but later relented under pressure from former guerrilla comrades that he run for congress, helping establish a large popular base within the province. Magsaysay's leadership by example–developed during his days as a guerrilla leader–characterized his other main attribute. Quirino secured the presidency aided by millions of pesos donated grudgingly by Chinese businessmen under pressure from the KMT-controlled Chinese chambers of commerce in Manila.

In less than a year, Magsaysay was made Secretary of National Defense. The US took a gamble by backing a man who was capable of developing such a large, popular base of support. Compounding the American gamble was that they were sponsoring Magsaysay against the vested interests of the existing establishment, an entirely new modus operandi for Americans.

Lansdale's guidance from Washington was sufficiently broad to provide him leeway to execute his mission as necessary, but it also had a clear intent to guide his actions. His mission was to: Protect American interests in the Philippines and to consolidate a power base for Ramon Magsaysay…, provide counsel and support to the new secretary of national defense, influence the revitalization of the Philippine Army, help the government make progress in its war against the Huks, urge political reform upon the government, and… help Filipinos have an honest election in the November, 1951 balloting.

In order to accomplish his assigned tasks, Lansdale arrived as a nominal member of JUSMAG [The Joint US Military Assistance Group to the Republic of the Philippines], ostensibly assigned as the intelligence advisor to President Quirino. In fact, his real authorities far exceeded his low rank and position. Embassy officials were supposed to cooperate with Lansdale almost without question, up to and including the ambassador and the JUSMAG chief. Despite Lansdale's significant power, the memories of Lansdale's colleagues at the embassy and in JUSMAG suggest that rather than abusing or flaunting his power, he preferred instead to build consensus and support for his operations.

The embassy and JUSMAG knew the AFP [Armed Forces of the Philippines] and PC needed new leadership, but they could only advise and apply pressure through aid. Now, with Magsaysay as Secretary of National Defense they had an ally in position to affect change. He needed broad authority from President Quirino to make personnel decisions if he was going to make the necessary reforms within the security forces; without them, he would be impotent.

Lansdale and the Americans were able to pressure President Quirino into giving Magsaysay more power, and his new powers were not insignificant. As a result, Magsaysay had the power to promote, demote, and fire, officers on the spot. Magsaysay insisted that field officers with good combat records take priority. The soldiers in the field now felt they had a champion in Manila. Morale steadily improved in the AFP, as did combat performance.

Another basic important initiative was increasing the pay of Filipino soldiers. Previously, AFP personnel only received 30 centavos a day. Magsaysay increased it to one peso a day, funded by US military aid. Magsaysay knew that his soldiers had been stealing food and other basic necessities from the populace, alienating the AFP from the people. The more than threefold increase in pay allowed soldiers to pay for supplies. As a result, esprit de corps gradually returned to the armed forces along with respect from the people.

Lansdale and Magsaysay had a daunting task to accomplish. Before they could reverse Huk successes, they had to find a way to rebuild the relationship between citizen and government. They had to identify ways to regain popular support and trust in the AFP. It was not simply a question of increasing military effectiveness against the Huks as the old-school Asia hands believed. Magsaysay's internal reforms were gaining traction, but it was an uphill battle against an entrenched establishment, that would take time. They needed to develop programs that would begin siphoning away the Huk support base, improve the AFP image, and alleviate the conditions of the Filipino people.

From the beginning, Magsaysay and the AFP embarked on a campaign to professionalize the Civilian Guards by sending AFP personnel to train and control them. The program must have been successful; former Huks credited Magsaysay with getting rid of the corrupt and inept Civilian Guards entirely. Lansdale also played an instrumental role in helping Magsaysay refine and develop his ideas further, in a unique way. Informal discussion groups developed at Lansdale's residence on Camp Murphy, where Magsaysay likewise lived. These groups grew to include AFP officers from combat units, staff officers, businessmen, trusted politicians, and essentially anyone Lansdale and Magsaysay thought might have innovative and useful ideas.

With popular trust and confidence in the AFP on the rise, the military campaign gained in-step traction against the Huks. Partnering with the Philippine Electoral Commission, Magsaysay and the AFP provided much needed manpower to the woefully understrength government body. Members of Lansdale's OPC team helped establish NAMFREL [National Movement for Free Elections] a non-governmental body dedicated to supporting clean elections through educating the electorate.

Lansdale also orchestrated a large national and international media turnout at polling sites to cover the election, further preventing fraud. The people came to appreciate that they now had a stake in their own government, Magsaysay's AFP was seen as having provided them the opportunity to exercise their rights. The Huk high water mark came and went with the 1951 election; but Magsaysay was rapidly moving from an inconvenience for Quirino to a potential rival. Magsaysay made approaches to Claro M. Recto and Lorenzo Tañada, suggesting that he should run as the opposition candidate for president in 1953. In at least one of these meetings, Lansdale was present.

On November 18, 1952, Magsaysay reassured Quirino that "I will betray my father before I will betray you."

Nevertheless, two days later Magsaysay signed a secret agreement with Recto, Laurel, and Tañada to the effect that he would run against Quirino on the Nacionalista ticket. Such is politics.

In little more than a year, Magsaysay and Lansdale achieved significant success in establishing the initiatives that formed the bottom-up effort to the Huk campaign. Magsaysay and Lansdale also succeeded in empowering the electorate, something the lower classes were denied following independence in 1946. The two men were able to achieve this–despite an entrenched and experienced political elite–because of their understanding of that elite and what it would take to counter them largely because of Lansdale's ability to build consensus rather than compel support.

With the turn of the new year in 1952, the Philippine government was making significantly greater inroads against the Huks, largely thanks to the efforts of Ramon Magsaysay and his supporters, and Edward Lansdale and the US embassy team. Furthermore, by empowering the electorate, Magsaysay represented a threat to the entrenched establishment. The next two years would require even more unity of effort within the American team at the embassy and support from Washington to counter Philippine establishment attempts to rid themselves of Magsaysay.

Just as the AFP was experiencing a renaissance under Magsaysay, the Huks were experiencing infighting and confusion amongst their ranks. Under PKP [*The Partido Komunista ng Pilipinas*-1930 (PKP-1930)–the Philippine Communist Party], the Huks were only ostensibly communist and subject to communist doctrine and theory; but outside of the senior leadership, the PKP-Huk union lacked theoretical and doctrinal depth.

Just as the AFP was regaining popular support within the populace during the November, 1951 elections, the Huks were preoccupied with their internal matters to their detriment. In September, 1952 Taruc issued a "Call for Peace," that while continuing to espouse the PKP line, further divided Huks in the field and the PKP leadership.

With regard to its long-term plans for Magsaysay, the CIA established and funded the NAMFREL in August, 1951. Gabriel Kaplan was recruited by the CIA and brought from New York "to help Lansdale elect Magsaysay president two years before the election was to take place."

One innovation that had a significant impact on the campaign was the creation of the scout ranger teams. The idea originated from a young Filipino lieutenant during brainstorming sessions at Magsaysay and Lansdale's combined residence. He broached the idea of forming small teams of highly trained personnel who would take the fight into the heart of Huk territories to conduct reconnaissance, raids, and ambushes, in areas the Huks once thought secure.

Complimentary to AFP offensive operations was the inclusion of psychological operations, or psywar—a favorite of Lansdale. Psyops were included into some aspect of almost every AFP operation. Lansdale's psychological operations focused on Huk morale in an attempt to get them to surrender. Lansdale was acting as Magsaysay's Svengali or *eminence gris*, tutoring the Defense secretary in the art of psychological warfare. Even though they had been largely responsible for creating his public image; in private, Lansdale and Bohannon characterized Magsaysay as a "superstitious, malleable pawn of their own creation."

It came as no surprise that the growing popularity and media coverage of Magsaysay's civic initiatives deepened Quirino's resentment. The entrenched political establishment was growing increasingly hostile to Magsaysay as well. He threatened their empire of greed. Possibly Magsaysay's initiatives were not politically motivated at the time they were instituted, but they definitely developed his popular support base. By the fall of 1952, popular feelings were expressed by visitors to Magsaysay's quarters; and Lansdale noted overwhelmingly positive public reaction to Magsaysay in areas that had once been solidly Huk territory.

Despite broad powers to prosecute the Huk campaign—including initiating governmental rights to habeas corpus–Magsaysay reversed the previous trend of the campaign that ignored civil rights. This approach further demonstrated to the masses that someone within the government was attempting to alter the unpopular status quo. It also further antagonized the self-absorbed elites and their entrenched political establishment. A showdown was brewing.

Magsaysay developed an effective reconciliation and reintegration program for surrendered Huks—another thorn in the incumbents' feet. Magsaysay and Lansdale both made frequent reference to the number of Huks who surrendered compared to the number of killed or captured as an example of the effectiveness of their campaign. Secretary Magsaysay believed the hard-core communists within the Huks had to be destroyed militarily, but rehabilitation remained his main course of action for the rest.

Magsaysay's rehabilitation policy was the EDCOR resettling program. Lansdale probably intended to use EDCOR for its psychological value, but Magsaysay saw it as building new communities in which the former Huks would rejoin society by working alongside fellow Filipinos. Edward Lansdale's team–code named *Kugown*–continued to focus on defeating the Huks militarily. However, he also pursued ways to promote his friend. Lansdale's team continued to focus on getting into the provinces to see conditions for themselves.

The entrenched political establishment alerted to Lansdale's efforts, and by the summer of 1952, Quirino was increasingly hostile towards the American. Nationalista Party leaders seized the opportunity almost immediately. They approached Magsaysay quietly to offer him the presidency on the Nationalista ticket. Part of their rationale was that with Magsaysay on the ticket, the AFP would not be used against them during the election. William Lacy at the US embassy believed that if Quirino felt sufficiently threatened, he might resort to authoritarian measures, such as declaring martial law, or jailing political opponents.

In keeping with the old-Asia hands close arrangement with the incumbent government, it made sure Lansdale was publicly no longer welcome in the JUSMAG. Edward was reassigned to the 13th Air Force's office of the historian at Clark Air Base north of Manila—a sharp comedown. But, Lansdale continued to run Magsaysay's campaign covertly, i.e. to follow his real orders. Regardless of his new cover, Quirino and his associates scrutinized Lansdale more than ever.

Magsaysay took advantage of President Quirino's harshly negative statement about Magsaysay's abilities to provide the perfect cover to allow Magsaysay to resign ahead of the planned Nationalista Party convention scheduled for March. During the convention, the party announced Magsaysay as their candidate for president. With the announcement of Magsaysay's candidacy, all eyes turned to the elections in November, clouded by comparison to memories of the 1949 elections.

There was little disagreement by anyone about the importance of the 1953 elections. Quirino and the Liberal Party saw the election as either an opportunity to reinstate the status quo ante, or the end of their monopoly on power. The Huks most likely saw it as an opportunity to keep

Magsaysay out of power and further undermine popular confidence in the government. The Americans and the opposition–led by Magsaysay–saw it as the opportunity to keep the democratic process alive in the Philippines.

All the progress made against the Huks could be undone if the 1953 elections went the way of the 1949 elections. Lansdale's own assessment of the situation–in his after-action report to the CIA about the elections–was severe, "if the Liberals had robbed the election there would have been a revolution, led by Magsaysay."

The US knew it had to tread carefully with Magsaysay. Any widespread conviction that he was hand-picked candidate of US would not further his political career. Ironically, by stating that the United States would only cooperate with a non-communist and that an administration elected through coercion would not receive aid, Acting Secretary of state Bruce was advocating intervention albeit obliquely. In order to avoid discovery of US intervention, support for Magsaysay had to come from Lansdale's team, with peripheral assistance from embassy assets. In Lansdale's opinion, if the US was going to defeat communism in the Philippines, they had no alternative but to support Magsaysay's campaign.

Despite having a clear bias, Lansdale directed his efforts and those of his team toward ensuring a fair election. They faced an entrenched elite that was shocked and dismayed that the lower classes actually wanted to vote as they pleased. The Papal Nuncio of the Philippines, Signor Emilio Vagnozzi, lent support to the Magsaysay campaign through the Catholic Church's voter education program, Catholic Action. With trustworthy support in place, Lansdale's team reinvigorated the organizations they built for the 1951 election and built relationships with other groups to diversify their outreach.

Lansdale's carefully chosen subordinates worked hard to ensure NAMFREL played an even bigger role during the 1953 election than it did in the 1951 election. The result was that the organization "gained strength in the first half of 1953, emerging prior to election day as a highly respected national body [candidates and citizens alike turned to it for impartial help]," he said.

The MPM [Magsaysay for President Movement–a group of business and professional people headed by Terry Adevoso] was active in building grassroots support for their candidate. By the time of the election the MPM had chapters in 15,600 of the approximately 18,000 barrios in the Philippines. The press played an important role in the 1951 elections, and Lansdale was intent on repeating that successful relationship with a useful ally. The Americans also established their own newspaper, *The Free Philippines*. Lansdale's preparations for the election and support for Magsaysay's campaign focused on educating the populace and ensuring a fair election.

Magsaysay—unlike Quirino and his elite Liberal Party cronies–engaged with the electorate everywhere he went; he took the time to stop and connect with individual Filipinos.

However–in a letter from Lansdale to Cowen about the campaign–he informed Cowen that:

> "You would thoroughly enjoy the way friend Ramon campaigns. You recall what a lousy public speaker he is. Well, he's knocking around in the barrio circuit in jeeps, trucks, caratelas, and carabao carts mostly shaking hands with people and talking only a few minutes…simple stuff, sure, but the people eat it up, understand it, and feel that here is one of them–far more than the big words that [Carlos Romulo] uses or the 'economic mobilization' words of Quirino."

In addition to Quirino's manipulation of the AFP and his clandestine overtures to the Huk, he sought to tamper directly with the ballots. Magsaysay's US-funded campaign was not averse to dirty tricks either: General Ralph Lovett–SAC of the CIA's Manila station–reported that the incumbent was drugged before he delivered a speech, rendering him incoherent. The election became a three-horse race with the entry of the "sugar bloc" team of Carlos Romulo and Quirino's vice-president, Fernando Lopez, who ran under the banner of the Democratic/Progressive which probably served to divide the vote between Qurino and Lopez.

In August, that team withdrew, with Romulo announcing that he would be supporting Magsaysay. The effect of this was to split the Liberal vote. A CIA operative heavily implied that Lopez was persuaded to join the Romulo team due to the fact that the CIA's Manila station had tape-recorded evidence of his extra-marital activity.

Given the massive publicity machine that had built Magsaysay's candidacy, it was obviously only the Liberals who would have an interest in rigging the election. And thus, the NAMFREL workers—who were fighting for free and honest elections–actually became Magsaysay activists by default.

Magsaysay was not entirely on the side of the angels. In the event of a fraudulent Quirino victory, he planned to stage a coup with US assistance. In the event, however, as "America's Boy", he won with a predictably overwhelming 69 percent of the vote. He was raised to the presidency for a specific purpose, in part to defeat the Huks. In an extreme case, US military authorities ordered the release of a disarmed Huk squadron 5,000 of collaborators, many of them from the political and elite establishment. The released unit was detained by a USAFF-recognized unit in Malolos, Pampanga Province and summarily executed. The leader of the unit was quickly arrested by the Americans and then quickly released and appointed mayor of Malolos. Huk leaders–including Luis Taruc–were quickly arrested and held by the US.

Within days of his election, Magsaysay met US Navy Secretary Robert Anderson, and in the following month, Anderson was able to tell a press conference in Washington that the Philippines "would be receptive toward granting the United States permanent use of the bases there".

Once Lansdale had installed Ngo Dinh Diem in South Vietnam, Magsaysay was among the very first to recognize the new regime: Claro M. Recto ascribed this to one factor:

"It was the arrival in Manila, accompanying the Chairman of Diem's Revolutionary Junta, of Colonel Edward Lansdale. He came, he saw, he spoke, and the President's last line of resistance easily snapped, and Lansdale walked away in triumph: He could still compel obedience."

–Claro Recto

But…, the purpose for which Magsaysay had been "invented" by Lansdale extended far beyond the Philippines, for the CIA's Manila station was using Filipinos to "spread democracy throughout SEATO [the Southeast Asia Treaty Organization] security area our Secretary of State had put together in Southeast Asia.

It was believed that the Filipinos would be more readily accepted than Americans in roles as political advisers and liaison officers with local intelligence services."

The Freedom Company of the Philippines was established by Lansdale in 1954, with Magsaysay as the company's honorary president. Its aim was to deploy Filipinos to Vietnam and elsewhere, being ostensibly a public service organization under contract to the host government.

… Freedom Company personnel assisted in drafting South Vietnam's constitution, trained the Vietnamese president's Guard Battalion, organized the Vietnamese Veterans' Legion to tie in with one of Cord Meyer's schemes to use veterans groups internationally as an anti-Communist front, and ran the huge Operation Brotherhood activity... The USA's 'fateful entanglement' in Vietnam began in Manila in the early 1950s, not in Saigon in the early sixties."

–CIA SAC, Manila, Joseph Smith

For all of Quirino's schemes, Lansdale still achieved his goal. In November, 1953, the Filipino people elected Ramon Magsaysay President of the Philippine Republic by an overwhelming majority: 2,912,992 to Quirino's 1,313,991. Edward Lansdale was later dubbed "General Landslide" for his part in Magsaysay's election to the presidency. Without a trace of irony, Washington's man in the Philippines reported:

"…my plan for a free election was approved …"

– CIA's Edward Lansdale

By the time Ramon Magsaysay assumed office in late December, 1953; Magsaysay and Lansdale's operations had also reduced the Huk support base to almost nothing; and Huk fighters were surrendering in ever increasing numbers because of the lure of Magsaysay's reconciliation policies. The level of US support Magsaysay enjoyed from 1950-1954 virtually evaporated overnight. Absent the PKP-Huk menace, US policy makers no longer felt the need to push for reforms behind the scenes.

A short time later, Edward Lansdale returned to the United States, his mission in the Philippines complete. The Eisenhower administration had already shifted focus to the communist threat in Vietnam, generally leaving Magsaysay and the Philippines to fend for themselves.

**Vietnam-**

The SMM [Saigon Military Mission] was born in a Washington policy meeting early in 1954, when Dien Bien Phu was still holding out against the encircling Vietminh. The SMM was to enter into Vietnam quietly and assist the Vietnamese–rather than the French–in unconventional warfare. The French were to be kept as friendly allies in the process, as far as possible.

In December, 1953–during a meeting convened in the Pentagon to discuss Vietnam–Secretary of State John Foster Dulles turned to Lansdale and told him, "We're going to send you over there."

Lansdale replied immediately, "Not to help the French!"

No, he was reassured, he would help the Vietnamese put down the Communist-dominated Viet Minh in Indochina. Allen Dulles, director of the Central Intelligence Agency, joined with his brother in backing Lansdale to serve as the founder and chief of the CIA's SMM [Saigon Military Mission], which was to enter Vietnam quietly and help the pro-Western Vietnamese wage political-psychological warfare. In 1953, Lansdale was sent to Vietnam temporarily to advise the French in their struggle with the Vietminh. Dulles told President Dwight Eisenhower that he was sending one of his "best men". Lansdale and a team of twelve intelligence agents were sent to Saigon. The SMM operative wrote a manual, *Operations of a 'Cold War' Combat Team*, compiled by the team itself in the field, little by little in moments taken as the members could. There are other teams in the field, American, French, British, Chinese, Vietnamese, Vietminh, and others. Each has its own story to tell.

The Saigon Military Mission started on June 1, 1954, when its Chief, Colonel Edward G. Lansdale, USAF, arrived in Saigon with a small box of files and clothes and a borrowed typewriter, courtesy of an SA-16 flight set up for him by the 13th Air Force at Clark AFB. Lt-General John O'Daniel and Embassy Chargé d'affaires Rob McClintock had arranged for his appointment as Assistant Air Attache, since it was improper for US officers at MAAG at that time to have advisory conferences with Vietnamese officers. Ambassador Heath had concurred already. There was no desk space for an office, no vehicle, no safe for files.

A bit annoyed at his last-minute orders to proceed directly from the Philippines to Vietnam–with no time to return home to Washington to prepare for his new covert mission or to visit his family—Colonel Edward Lansdale flew into Saigon in the rattling bucket seat of an amphibian aircraft from the 31st Air-Sea Rescue Squadron. It was the first available flight out of Clark Air Force Base to Saigon, and the crewmen agreed to take him if he did not mind the extra flight time while they performed their patrol over the South China Sea. It was June 1, 1954; and as he sipped coffee from a paper cup, he thought about what lay ahead. He had heard about the French defeat at Dien Bien Phu and knew that the French and Viet Minh were working out a peace settlement in Geneva—but beyond that—his knowledge about the country was slim.

After Landing at Tan Son Nhut air base in Saigon, Lansdale hitched a ride into the heart of the city to the home of Lt. Gen. John W. "Iron Mike" O'Daniel, who was the post chief of the MAAG [Military Assistance Advisory Group] in Saigon. The MAAG had been established in 1950 by President Harry Truman to work with French forces in Indochina.

Lansdale's selection as the man to run paramilitary and political operations against the Viet Minh in Indochina should not have come as too much of a surprise to the dapper 46-year-old O'Daniel, however. After all, Lansdale had served the previous year as a psychological warfare adviser on an evaluation team tour of French Indochina, headed by General O'Daniel. Lansdale's observations—recorded in several memoranda on the nature of Asiatic insurgencies—dissected the Communists' successful tactics, and underscored the French and American lack of fluency regarding counterinsurgency.

"There is general conviction that the Viet Minh has 'national spirit' on its side and that the Franco-Vietnamese forces do not… This is the result of successful psychological-political warfare by the Viet Minh. There has been no effective psychological warfare by the Franco-Vietnamese forces to expose this as a myth."

–Colonel Edward Lansdale

Lansdale was intent on understanding and applying the psychological aspects of warfare against Communists that he had learned from the fight against the Communist Huks. In Indochina, he aimed to use black propaganda and urge the French and their Vietnamese allies to seize the initiative in countering the Viet Minh's hold over the people.

In Saigon, Lansdale took on the cover of an assistant air attaché at the US Embassy, an arrangement that allowed him to work with both the ambassador, Donald Heath, and General O'Daniel's MAAG. When Lansdale announced himself at the embassy, however, the diplomatic staff was indignant; the SMM was not the only CIA operation in town. A regular CIA station–responsible for traditional intelligence and spying– also existed, separate from Lansdale's unit.

The station chief, Emmett McCarthy, considered Lansdale to be an amateur. McCarthy insisted on control of all secret communications with Washington, and Lansdale had to comply because he had no independent communications channel. An intense rivalry developed. Eventually–after Lansdale quietly complained to Secretary of State Dulles about him–a more amicable station chief, John Anderton, replaced McCarthy. From that point on, Lansdale was almost always referred to as "the Chief" in dispatches and in person.

For the first month after arriving in Saigon, Colonel Lansdale was the entire SMM staff. Then on July 1, Major Lucien Conein–an experienced covert operator who had been in the OSS and who had jumped into Vietnam to help guerrilla forces fight the Japanese during World War II– joined Lansdale's team.

But the Chief faced some daunting challenges. Since Ho Chi Minh proclaimed the Independent Democratic Republic of Vietnam in September, 1945, the xenophobic Vietnamese had only two choices: Support Ho's Viet Minh republic or their French colonial masters. Addressing this, the French had created a partially autonomous government, called the State of Vietnam, headed by the aging playboy emperor Bao Dai. Although it had a governing body called the Chamber of Deputies, none of its members had any real constituency. Most Vietnamese hated the French and felt little loyalty to Bao Dai, who lived in France.

As the Geneva negotiations–which had convened in early May coinciding with the fall of Dien Bien Phu–progressed, the State of Vietnam's French and American backers scrambled to shore up its legitimacy and capability. Ngo Dinh Diem, a well-known Catholic, anti-Communist nationalist residing in Europe, was appointed by Bao Dai—with US support—as prime minister on June 16.

The day after Diem's arrival in Saigon on June 25, Lansdale paid a visit and presented the new prime minister with an unofficial, "personal" paper full of actions he could take to handle the rapidly changing situation in his country. The Chief's ideas included immediate steps to integrate all non-Communist military and paramilitary forces into a national army, encouragement of nationalist groups to participate in the political process, and the institution of agrarian and economic reforms, to make the government more responsive and effective.

As his aide translated the letter to the prime minister, Lansdale recalled, "Diem listened intently, asked some searching questions, thanked me for my thoughtfulness, folded up the paper, and put it in his pocket."

Thus, as he had done with the Philippine leader Magsaysay, Lansdale quickly gained Diem's trust and became his closest American confidant.

Despite having developed a friendship, it was still altogether unclear how the newbie, Lansdale, could assist Diem in setting up a unified nationalist government in the south when none of the hundreds of sects, with their clandestine organizations, competing ideologies, and armed camps, could become interested in supporting a new government? Lansdale knew that Diem initially controlled virtually nothing and needed to solidify his grip on power quickly and improve the functioning of his government and thereby enhance his popularity.

Realizing that the army was the strongest and the only unifying factor in bringing a nationalist government to Vietnam, Lansdale set to work, conferring with officials such as Defense Minister Phan Huy Quat and General Nguyen Van Hinh, chief of staff of the Vietnamese National Army. Lansdale became an unofficial adviser to Captain Pham Xuan Giai, head of G5 [5th Bureau, the psychological warfare department of the Vietnamese army general staff and immediately set about to establish a school to train the Vietnamese troops in psywar as well as to enhance their image among the Vietnamese people.

Lansdale fervently believed it was necessary for Diem's government to appeal directly to the Vietnamese population, and he planned to employ classic psywar tactics to enhance those efforts.

"If the Viet Minh have sold the idea of being anti-French, the Vietnamese can sell the idea of being anti-Chinese and prove that the Viet Minh are controlled by Chinese," he had written in a memorandum.

Lansdale was convinced that the Viet Minh had waged a successful psychological campaign by word-of-mouth, and he was determined to counteract it through the use of his own word-of-mouth rumors, black leaflets, and other psywar methods. The new colonel also believed that he would be able to convert many of the Vietnamese who had fought with the Viet Minh against the French but who did not necessarily want to be Communist—they just wanted French rule to end. That was Lansdale's attitude, and also that of his president, John F. Kennedy, and Kennedy's predecessors, Franklin D. Roosevelt, Harry S. Truman, and Dwight D. Eisenhower.

Meanwhile–at the Geneva Conference–the French and the Ho Chi Minh's Communists finally reached an accommodation on July 21, 1954. With the effective cease-fire date of August 11, the US military personnel ceiling was to be frozen at its existing number. Lansdale had to scramble to beat the deadline to beef up his SMM. Word quickly went out and 17 additional CIA officers were recruited, including Army Lt. Col. Gordon Jorgenson as Lansdale's second-in-command. Many of these recruits held rank in the US military as well as the CIA and had experience in paramilitary and clandestine intelligence operations. However, Lansdale grumbled that no one except himself had served in psywar operations. Lansdale was a worker, and he realized how much he would have to do.

"I still had no office, but I had been assigned a small bungalow on Rue Miche near the heart of town the week before," Lansdale wrote in his autobiography. "Gathering my newcomers at the bungalow, I described the situation to them. They were to be trainers in counter guerrilla warfare, but the French had yet to give permission for US training of the Vietnamese in subjects known by the team. They would have to be patient and wait."

The Chief split his staff in half and put Conein in charge of the SMM team sent north, which would temporarily operate out of Hanoi with two objectives: develop a paramilitary organization that would be in place once the Viet Minh took over; and sabotage the Communist government. The southern team based in Saigon focused on trying to help Diem establish a stable government. Working in close cooperation with George Hellyer, USIS Chief, a new psychological warfare campaign was devised for the Vietnamese Army and for the government in Hanoi.

The Geneva Accords stipulated the cease-fire, a phased disengagement of the French Union and Viet Minh forces, and the 17th Parallel was established as a dividing point. The Viet Minh would regroup north of the line, and the French forces would regroup in the south. With the French departure, the united State of Vietnam was to become fully independent. After a period of two years, a unified national election would be held in 1956 that would determine the governance of all of Vietnam, north and south. Ho Chi Minh was confident he could win in such an election, but the French and Americans believed that Geneva's two-year window would give them the time needed to build a viable nation in the south that could win over enough of the Vietnamese to elect a Diem-led government—one that would be open to US influence.

The Geneva Accords' Article 8 was key to achieving that goal. It declared that for a period of 300 days everyone in Vietnam could freely decide "in which zone he wishes to live." Lansdale saw this as a "Geneva-given" chance for large numbers of Vietnamese to move from the north before the Communists took over. He hoped to be able to influence 2 million northerners to migrate to the south, giving Diem the upper hand in the Geneva-mandated 1956 vote. That espionage-based concept was to dominate US intelligence services' clandestine activity until the 1956 decision.

Lansdale set in motion a series of concurrent spy operations to affect his scheme for persuading northerners to move south. First, Lansdale and his SMM needed to convince them that their living conditions would soon deteriorate under Communist rule. Working closely with the US Information Service, Lansdale's team began a disinformation campaign wherein Vietnamese G-5 soldiers dressed in civilian clothes were sent north to local marketplaces to spread a rumor that the Viet Minh had made a deal to allow Chinese troops into the north again. They used every ruse and threat to convince the already discombobulated North Vietnamese that those Chinese troops were terrorizing the Vietnamese, raping women, and stealing, on a grand scale.

To help sell that idea, villagers were told about the Ho Chi Minh government also slaying thousands of political opponents in North Vietnam. Throughout the countryside, the villagers were reminded of how Chinese troops had behaved after World War II. Many of them became so frightened that they packed up and moved their large families south. The rumors were so convincing that Lansdale reportedly received a query from officials in Washington, asking him if there was any credence to the report that two Chinese regular divisions were in north Vietnam. The plan was for the story was to be planted by soldiers of the Vietnamese Armed Psywar Company in Hanoi dressed in civilian clothes. Those troops received their instructions silently, dressed in civilian clothes, went on the mission, and failed to return. They had deserted to the Vietminh. Murphy's Law in evidence. Nevertheless, weeks later, Tonkinese told an excited story of the misbehavior of the Chinese Divisions in Vietminh territory. Investigated, it turned out to be the old rumor campaign, with Vietnamese embellishments.

Building on the semi-successful rumor campaign, the SMM started printing and covertly distributing "black leaflets" that were purportedly from the Viet Minh. These leaflets gave instructions to citizens on how they should conduct themselves when the Viet Minh takeover of Hanoi occurred in October. Included in the disinformation was the Viet Minh's program for "monetary reform." The leaflet ignited anxiety that gained momentum among the populace.

Within two days of the leaflet's distribution, the Viet Minh currency fell to half its previous value. At the same time, the number of North Vietnamese registering to emigrate south tripled. The Viet Minh leadership–which quickly understood what was happening–took to the airwaves to denounce the bogus leaflets. But–as a testament to the effectiveness of the ruse–many Viet Minh and their supporters were convinced that the Communists' radio denunciations themselves were actually a psychological warfare trick undertaken by the French.

Not only did this one black leaflet sabotage the Viet Minh currency, it also subverted Viet Minh population-control efforts. More importantly, it also managed to throw rank and file Viet Minh cadre into a state of confusion and disarray—just weeks before they were to assume control of Hanoi. Ho Chi Minh's government and army were rapidly becoming embroiled in chaos.

The northern SMM team under Conein organized a paramilitary group–disguised by the Vietnamese name of Binh–through the Northern

Dai Viets, a political party with loyalties to Bao Dai. The group was to be trained and supported by the US as patriotic Vietnamese, to come eventually under government control when the government was ready for such activities. Thirteen Binhs were quietly exfiltrated through the port of Haiphong–under the direction of Lt. Andrews– and taken on the first stage of the journey to their training area by a US Navy ship. This was the first of a series of helpful actions by Task Force 98, commanded by Admiral Sabin.

Another extremely effective SMM project aimed at convincing northerners to migrate capitalized on the widespread Vietnamese belief in astrology and superstition. That scam leveraged on Lansdale's background in communications and advertising. Noting the popularity of soothsayers among the general populace and an absence of any publication that carried their predictions, he struck on the idea of printing an almanac of predictions for 1955 from well-known astrologers and noted fortunetellers. His team sought out and paid leading Vietnamese astrologers to make predictions about coming disasters that would transpire coincident with the Viet Minh takeover of northern Vietnam.

The astrologers' almanac predicted prosperity for those in the south and convincingly foretold of hardship and calamity in the north, including bloody reprisals against villagers resisting Viet Minh economic and agrarian reforms. These almanacs were smuggled deep into Viet Minh territory by the SMM spies–and to enhance their credibility–they were offered for sale rather than distributed for free. As Lansdale predicted, they were then passed along throughout the north, and the almanac proved to be an especially big seller in the main refugee port of Haiphong. Indeed, the almanac proved to be so popular among the Vietnamese that it had a second printing and turned a profit, which Lansdale used to subsidize his other operations.

Knowing firsthand the power of the press, Lansdale sought to destroy the largest printing presses in Hanoi; and in September the northern SMM team raced to the site, only to find that the Viet Minh had already placed security guards at the plant.

In an effort to destabilize the north's infrastructure, Conein's people in Hanoi worked to sabotage the transportation systems—contaminating the oil supply of the city's bus company and taking initial action to impair of the north's railroad system. Lansdale also wanted to sabotage the north's power and water plants, and its harbors and bridges; but US adherence to the Geneva Accords prevented such action much to Lansdale's dissatisfaction. At least, the team compiled detailed notes to use for future paramilitary operations against those potential targets. Conein's team left Hanoi along with the last French troops to depart the city on October 9, 1954.

To discourage northward migration from the south, the SMM concocted another black leaflet–purporting to originate with the Viet Minh Resistance Committee–that was distributed in southern Viet Minh zones by Vietnamese National Army soldiers disguised as civilians.

The very genuine appearing leaflet helpfully informed people heading to northern Vietnam that "they would be kept safe below decks from imperialist air and submarine attacks." The missive also instructed refugees to bring warm clothing with them. The "warm clothing" reference was then carefully coupled with a word–of–mouth rumor campaign that Viet Minh were being sent into China to work as railroad laborers.

Lansdale wanted Viet Minh supporters to remain south of the 17th Parallel voluntarily; so, they could be "re-educated later." He also hoped— by getting their families to resist—to stop the abduction of other young men to the north by the Viet Minh.

The vast majority of the Vietnamese Catholics lived in the north, and many of them required little convincing to move south for a new start under the anti-Communist Catholic Diem. But Lansdale took no chances and the strength of the northerners' Catholicism. For those on the fence, the SMM spread rumors that Catholics would be arrested and executed in the north, and that even "the Blessed Virgin Mary had gone south." For many that was the most convincing argument and the final straw to get them to move in large numbers into Diem's South Vietnam.

In the end—prior to the Geneva Convention's 1956 deadline, the SMM efforts contributed to a massive flow of northerners to the south. An estimated 900,000 sought transport to the south, which in turn led to a huge refugee problem as thousands of registrants flooded the Haiphong port for passage. This situation provided Lansdale another prime opportunity to get international publicity and support. Ultimately, several nations volunteered to provide assistance and–along with ships of the US Seventh Fleet, transported refugees south in "Operation Passage to Freedom."

Lansdale hastened the departure of the northerners as the deadline approached by dropping leaflets in the Northern hamlets stating that "Christ has gone to the South" and other black leaflets showing maps with concentric circles emanating from Hanoi suggesting an imminent nuclear bomb strike on the Northern capital.

Lancaster's efforts to stem south to north flow of Vietnamese was highly successful. Only ~90,000 people left southern Vietnam for the north. In addition—as if to rub salt into Ho Chi Minh's wounds–the SMM took advantage of the northbound refugee flow to facilitate infiltration of Vietnamese agents who had been trained for future operations against the Hanoi government. The movements of the paramilitary teams and their supplies were made under the pretense of working with refugees. Lansdale's SMM was successful in smuggling men and supplies from Saigon to sites in the north.

As the Chief saw it, this massive influx to the south had a material effect on the Geneva-mandated Vietnam-wide plebiscite specified for the summer of 1956. Ultimately, while Lansdale fell short of the 2 million he hoped for, the transfer served to bring the populations of northern and southern Vietnam into closer balance, at about 12 million apiece.

Colonel Lansdale also recruited mercenaries from the Philippines to carry out acts of sabotage in North Vietnam. This was unsuccessful and most of the mercenaries were arrested and put on trial in Hanoi. Finally, Lansdale set about training ARVN [the South Vietnamese army] in modem fighting methods, since it was becoming clear that it was only a matter of time before the communists would resort to open warfare.

Throughout all his spy activities in the north, Landsdale never lost sight of his most important mission–to solidify Diem's grip on power and improve the functioning of his government. Seemingly indefatigable, Lansdale worked diligently to coerce and bribe many of Diem's southern opponents into at least tacit support for the new south Vietnamese leader. He thwarted a plan by the Vietnamese National Army's chief of staff to launch a coup against Diem: in October, 1954, Lansdale foiled a coup attempt, cutting General Nguyễn Văn Hinh's communication off from his top lieutenants by moving them to Manila; and he made significant cash payments to several leaders of the Cao Dai and Hoa Hao sects to buy their support. The powerful Binh Xuyen criminal organization, which—with Bao Dai's consent— controlled much of Saigon, proved the most difficult to deal with.

Lansdale played a leading role in influencing key Cao Dai General Trinh Minh *Thế* into realigning with Diem after he had temporarily thrown his weight behind the criminal Binh Xuyen gang and the Cao Đài and Hòa Hảo religious sects in March, 1955. With Gen. *Thế*'s support, Diem sent the army into the Cholon area of Saigon in April and brutally crushed the sect gang and the sects. With that, the United States stopped wavering in its support of the Diem regime and strongly supported him thereafter. For Lansdale, it was a success comparable to his winning over his US superiors in support of Ramon Magsaysay in the Philippines.

As Diem's support and power in the south grew and solidified, he was emboldened to undermine and erode Bao Dai's political standing, and to make known his refusal to countenance the Geneva-mandated all-Vietnam election in 1956 that would likely pit himself against Ho Chi Minh for the presidency. Lansdale was encouraging Diem that his prospects in such an election were good, and Western allies were hopeful that it would be the Viet Minh that would pull out of the accord, but Diem had his own agenda.

On the anniversary of his installation as prime minister in July, Diem announced his intention to hold a referendum in October to determine the future of the country in the south. A week later—formally declaring a free and fair election with Communist participation was impossible— Diem proclaimed, "We will not be tied down by the [Geneva] treaty that was signed against the wishes of the Vietnamese people."

As a result, France-based Bao Dai removed Diem from his government, but was rendered impotent in Diem's political campaign against him. In early October, Diem announced the referendum, with himself and Bao Dai facing each other in the election, took place October 23.

Lansdale's overall campaign plan was to mount a propaganda campaign to persuade the Vietnamese people in the south not to vote for the communists in the forthcoming elections.In October, 1955, the South Vietnamese people were asked to choose between Bo Dai, the former

Emperor of Vietnam, and Ngo Dinh Diem for the leadership of the country. Lansdale suggested that Diem should provide two ballot papers, red for Diem and green for Bao Dai. Lansdale hoped that the Vietnamese belief that red signified good luck whilst green indicated bad fortune, would help influence the result.

When the voters arrived at the polling stations, they found Diem's supporters in attendance.

One voter complained afterwards: "They told us to put the red ballot into envelopes and to throw the green ones into the wastebasket. A few people, faithful to Bao Dai, disobeyed. As soon as they left, the agents went after them, and roughed them up... They beat one of my relatives to pulp."

They also threw out the green ballots.

After the election Ngo Dinh Diem informed his American advisers that he had achieved 98.2 per cent of the vote. Hoping for an outcome similar to Magsaysay's in the Philippines—a widely recognized fair election—Lansdale told Diem he would likely win overwhelmingly and that he should avoid rigging the vote. But that was not to be the case, and in an election fraught with intimidation and ballot stuffing, Diem emerged victorious with more than 98 percent of the vote. Lansdale tried to get Diem to announce something more reasonable, like around 70 percent, but Diem ignored the request. He was–thereafter viewed by most his and the American people as morally compromised and corrupt.

While the United States had little choice but to accept and support Diem, even Lansdale's immense efforts could not–in the long run– maintain American support for the leader in whom so much was invested. Data were produced that indicated that South Vietnam was undergoing an economic miracle. With the employment of $250 million of aid per year from the United States and the clever manipulating of statistics, it was reported that economic production had increased dramatically.

Ngo Dinh Diem would stand as America's imperfect anti-Communist mainstay in Saigon until his overthrow and assassination in November 1963—green lighted by the Kennedy administration.

Lansdale remained in Vietnam until the end of 1956. His departure for Vietnam from the Philippines, along with a significant number of his CIA team members, created a void there. A similar void occurred in Vietnam when his dynamic presence was no longer felt. In 1957–after brief staff duty with Headquarters, US Air Force–he was transferred in June, 1957 to the Office of the Secretary of Defense, with duties as deputy assistant to the secretary of defense for special operations. In 1959, he served on the staff of the President's Committee on Military Assistance [the Draper Committee]. He was given a temporary promotion to brigadier general in April, 1960. On February 24, 1961, he was appointed assistant to the secretary of defense as a major general, where his primary duties involve attention to special operations of an extremely sensitive nature.

He returned to Vietnam from 1965 to 1968 where he worked in the United States Embassy, Saigon, with the rank of minister. He was one of the first Americans to recognize the truly unconventional nature of the war in Vietnam, and his expertise in applied psychological warfare would not be matched by any other American officer. From an unusual lack of information for that period, it appears that the scope of his delegated authority was vague; and he was bureaucratically marginalized and frustrated.

Robert McNamara–secretary of defense from 1961 to 1968–demanded that Lansdale help in the overthrow and murder of Diem. Edward refused and McNamara summarily fired him, according to Lansdale's later memoirs. Edward Lansdale's SMM operation in Vietnam only became known to the public with the release of the Pentagon Papers and the declassification of other confidential Pentagon documents in 1971.

## Anti-Castro Campaign

### Background:

- January, 1960- The CIA set up a Task Force [WH-4, Branch 4 of the Western Hemisphere Division] to implement President Eisenhower's request for an ambitious covert program to overthrow the Castro government. Jacob Esterline, Guatemala station chief between 1954-1957 was in charge.
- January 12, 1960- Throughout the month of January, sabotage and small bombing missions in Cuba increased in frequency. A plane dropped incendiary bombs in the areas of Bainoa, Caraballo, and San Antonio de Rio Blanco. Another plane coming from the

north–with US markings–dropped inflammable material on cane fields next to the Hershey factory.

- January 18, 1960- A plane dropped live phosphorous over the cane plantations of Quemados de Guines and Rancho Veloz, in Las Villas. Seven people are detained in Sagua la Grande for trying to derail the Sagua/Havana train.
- January 21, 1960- A plane dropped four one-hundred-pound bombs on the urban district of Cojimar y Regla in Havana.
- January 25, 1960- President Eisenhower held a conference to discuss the situation in Cuba. "The President said that Castro begins to look like a madman."
- "[Castro] is a very conspiratorial individual who tries to create the impression that he and Cuba are beleaguered. He is an extreme Leftist and is strongly anti-American," Ambassador Bonsal, also at the conference, added.
- January 28, 1960- At 1600 in the afternoon in the town of Chambas on the north coast, a Catalina plane dropped incendiary bombs that failed to go off. The bombs have the inscription "Bristo Marines." Another plane dropped incendiary bombs on the cane fields in the refineries of Adelaida, Violeta, Patria, Punta Alegre, and Morón, in Camaguey; and Monati, Delicias, and Chapana, in Oriente. The incendiary devices dropped on central Adelaide almost totally destroy 40 million arrobas ["arroba"=25 pounds] of cane.
- January 29-31, 1960- A plane dropped incendiary phosphorous bombs on 10 districts in the area of the Chapana refinery. Other bombing attacks occurred on cane plantations in San Isidro and on houses in the Central Toledo in Havana. More than 100,000 arrobas of cane were burned in Alacranes and Jovellanos in the province of Matanzas.
- February, 1960- The MRR [Movimiento de Recuperación Revolucionaria] released its "Ideario" of basic points—"not only to overthrow Fidel Castro, but to permanently fight for an ideology of Christ; and for a reality of liberating our nation treacherously sold to the Communist International."

- February 17, 1960- A CIA briefing to the National Security Council reports on the visit of Soviet official Anastas Mikoyan to Cuba. "The USSR", it states, "has shifted from cautious attitude to one of active support." The briefing also indicates that opposition to Castro is growing but that "the anti-Castro groups both inside and outside the country lack organization and effective leadership." (CIA, Briefing, Cuba)
- February 18, 1960- A plane trying to bomb the central España, Matanzas province, explodes in mid-air. The pilot is identified as Robert Ellis Frost, an American who carries a U.S. military identification card.
- March, 1960- The CIA organized an operation in which it trained and funded a force of exiled counter-revolutionary Cubans serving as the armed wing of the Democratic Revolutionary Front, known as Brigade 2506.
- The Puzzle Palace began training 300 guerrillas, initially in the US and the Canal Zone. Following an agreement with President Ydígoras in June, training shifted to Guatemala. The CIA began work to install a powerful radio station on Greater Swan Island, ninety-seven miles off the coast of Honduras.
- March 4-5, 1960- Sabotage of a French ship, La Coubre, in Havana harbor, carrying arms for Cuba, kills about 100 people and wounds some 300. The following day at funerals for the victims Fidel Castro accuses the United States of responsibility for the action.
- March 17, 1960- At an Oval Office meeting with high-ranking national security officials, President Eisenhower approved a Central Intelligence Agency policy paper titled "A Program of Covert Action Against the Castro Regime" with four main courses of action: (1) form a moderate opposition group in exile whose slogan will be to restore the revolution which Castro has betrayed; (2) create a medium wave radio station to broadcast into Cuba, probably on Swan Island, south of Cuba; (3) create a covert intelligence and action organization within Cuba responsive to the orders and directions of the exile opposition; and (4) begin

training a paramilitary force outside Cuba and, in a second phase, train paramilitary cadres for immediate deployment into Cuba to organize, train, and lead, resistance forces recruited there.

President Eisenhower argued that everyone must be prepared to deny its existence and only two or three people should have contact with the groups involved, agitating Cubans to do most of what must be done. The President told Mr. Dulles to go ahead with the plan and the operations but that "our hand should not show in anything that is done."

- March 27, 1960- Following a tour of Latin America by Artíme to drum up support for MRR, Rafael Rivas-Vasquez wrote a letter on the status of the movement. "The problem is to get going… the letter states… the Americans have yet be fully supportive beyond saying, 'ok to everything.' If we show signs of life in Cuba… they will definitively give us help." (Handwritten letter, 3/27/60). The following day, Castro warned, "if there is an invasion, the war, they can be sure, will be to the death."

- Late March, 1960- David Atlee Phillips, a CIA contract employee who until recently had maintained a public-relations company in Havana, is selected by the CIA as chief of propaganda for the Cuba project. At operation headquarters in Washington, Phillips is told that the Cuba project will go by the Guatemala scenario. Phillips had performed the same function in PBSUCCESS, the 1954 operation against Guatemalan President Jacobo Arbenz. During that coup by a CIA directed exile force, Phillips had operated a clandestine station supporting them. CIA operative E. Howard Hunt–also a veteran of the Guatemala operation–was assigned the position of chief of political action for the project. His primary responsibility was to form a government-in-exile to replace Castro's government following the invasion.

- Mid-April, 1960- David Phillips meets with the CIA official in charge of the Cuba operation, Deputy Director for Plans Richard Bissell. When Bissell asks how long it will take to create the proper psychological climate, Phillips says it will take about six months. Bissell directs the propaganda chief to have Radio Swan up and running in one month.

On Swan Island–a tiny, contested territory located about 100 miles off Honduras–the CIA began construction of a 50 kilowatt medium-wave radio station. The island had served as a base for CIA broadcasting during the agency's successful campaign to oust Guatemala's President Arbenz, and some radio equipment used in that operation was still on the island. Phillips obtained a transmitter from the US Army in Germany, which was preparing to make it available to the Voice of America. A detachment of Navy Seabees constructed a pier at Swan Island to facilitate the unloading of the equipment.

- April 23, 1960- Cuba's Foreign Minister Raúl Roa declared, "I can guarantee categorically that Guatemalan territory is being used at this very time with the complicity of President Ydígoras and the assistance of United Fruit, as a bridgehead for an invasion of our country."
- May, 1960- CIA operative Howard Hunt spent several days in Cuba on an undercover visit, during which he observed Cuban attitudes toward the revolutionary government and visited areas around revolution controlled radio stations. After returning to Washington, he offered several recom-mendations, including a suggestion that the Agency destroy the Cuban radio and television transmitters before or coincident with the invasion. That recommendation was based on his belief that without radio and television to inform the country, Castro's heirs would be unable to rally mass support.
- May 7, 1960- Two US warplanes flew over Cuban territorial waters, close to the Cuban coast; and a US destroyer entered Cuban waters. Two other US warplanes flew over Cabo Cruz.
- May 12, 1960- Cuban forces brought down a Piper Apache plane near Mariel killing the pilot, a US citizen named Matthew Edward Duke.
- May 13,1960- President Eisenhower met with his advisers to discuss what to do about General Trujillo in the Dominican Republic. The conversation also touched upon dealing with Castro. Eisenhower comments that he would like to see Castro and Trujillo "both sawed off."

- May 19, 1960: A small group from Brigade 2506–housed by the CIA in the motel Marie Antonet in Fort Lauderdale–were met by Manuel Artíme and two CIA officials, "Jimmy and Karl." Jimmy was identified as the chief of the operation, and later as chief of the infiltration team. The team was subsequently transported to Ussepa Island off the Florida coast for training of Brigade 2506. Other members of the brigade arrived later and are assigned numbers. The training was originally scheduled to last 15 days but extended to a month and a half. In early July, the Brigadistas were transferred by plane to camps in Guatemala.
- May 30, 1960- Cuban security forces rounded up members of an internal resistance organization named the "Western Anticommunist Organization."
- Early July, 1960- Exile forces being trained on Ussepa Island are transferred to bases in Guatemala. There, "Mr. Karl,"–the CIA official in charge of the training– meets this group of exiles. Three Americans, "Bill, Bob and Nick," are in charge of training exile members in radio communications.
- August, 1960: Richard Bissell met with Colonel Sheffield Edwards– director of the CIA's Office of Security–to discuss ways to eliminate or assassinate Fidel Castro. Edwards proposed that the job be done by assassins handpicked by the American underworld, specifically syndicate interests who have been driven out of their Havana gambling casinos by the Castro regime. Bissell gave Edwards the go-ahead to proceed. Between August 1960, and April 1961–the CIA with the help of the Mafia–pursued a series of plots to poison or shoot Castro. The CIA's own internal report on these efforts states that these plots "were viewed by at least some of the participants as being merely one aspect of the overall active effort to overthrow the regime that culminated in the Bay of Pigs." (CIA, Inspector General's Report on Efforts to Assassinate Fidel Castro).

José Miró Cardona led the anti-Castro Cuban exiles in the United States. A former member of Castro's government, he was the head of the Cuban Revolutionary Council, an exile committee. Cardona was poised to take over the provisional presidency of Cuba if the invasion succeeded.

The failure of the Bay of Pigs invasion is the stuff of history and will only be mentioned here. The Bay of Pigs Invasion was a failed attack launched by the CIA in 1961 to push Cuban leader Fidel Castro from power. The invasion was financed and directed by the US government via the CIA on the orders of President John F. Kennedy. The attack was launched by 1,400 American-trained Cubans who had fled their homes when Castro took over. The invasion was doomed from the start, since the invaders were badly outnumbered by Castro's troops, CIA support was inadequate, the landing point at the Bay of Pigs—part of the deception—was a remote swampy area on the southern coast of Cuba, where a night landing might bring a force ashore against little resistance and help to hide any US involvement. Unfortunately, the landing site also left the invading force more than 80 miles from refuge in Cuba's Escambray Mountains, if anything went wrong.

When things did go wrong, reinforcement was denied by the Kennedy administration. They surrendered after less than 24 hours of fighting. The failed invasion strengthened the position of Castro's administration, which proceeded to proclaim its intention to adopt socialism and pursue closer ties with the Soviet Union openly. The failed invasion led to a reassessment of Cuba policy by the Kennedy administration. [Carl Douglass: Too little and too late.]

Whether or not Edward Lansdale was an advisor for the Bay of Pigs fiasco is uncertain, but the modus operandi smacks of his brand of dirty tricks. However, he was directly involved in the subsequent Operation Mongoose, a follow-up mission to correct the failures of the ill-conceived Bay of Pigs operation.]

## Brigadier General Edward Lansdale and OPERATION MONGOOSE-

Lansdale was pulled out of Saigon in 1956–after two years as President Diem's house guest and confidant–and kicked upstairs in Washington to the Office of the Secretary of Defense in 1957. There he served as Deputy Assistant Secretary for Special Operations. Over the next four years Lansdale quietly participated in both covert operations and military diplomacy. Although he generally operated under an appropriate cover, his reception by cronies and counterparts overseas occasionally made the nature of his activities quite transparent. Through his own flair for publicity, by 1960 he had become a celebrity-particularly in the Pacific.

President-elect Kennedy received one or more of Edward Lansdale's "think" papers on Vietnam and was roundly impressed by his advocacy of a "nonbureaucratic" approach to counterinsurgency. New President Kennedy concluded that Fidel Castro was a Soviet client posing a threat to all of Latin America. Kennedy's prompt approval just ten days after taking office of a new "Counterinsurgency Plan" for Vietnam–a shift away from a prior emphasis on a Korea-style threat to South Vietnam– suggested a more than casual acquaintance with the issues involved To the incoming Kennedy administration, there were few Americans more eminently qualified to advise on unconventional warfare and the American role in Indochina than Edward Geary Lansdale. Besides, Kennedy liked swashbuckling "think-on-your-feet" 007 types of black ops agents. Although Lansdale's reputation as a practical, sensitive counterinsurgent would be tarnished in the 1960s, his public legend would endure. General Lansdale was, in any case, one of the most influential of American counterinsurgents, and important if only because his role as a principal spanned the formative years of the doctrine, from the Philippines of the 1940s to Vietnam in the 1960s.

Upon taking office, Kennedy brought Lansdale to the White House for a meeting of top Pentagon, State Department, and National Security Officers, and–apparently to their horror–intimated there that Lansdale could be the next US ambassador to Saigon. The new administration's Undersecretary of Defense, Roswell Gilpatric, reminiscing on his dealings with Lansdale years later for an archive oral history project, explained that although Lansdale was an outcast with his military peers, and perhaps even less esteemed by the State Department, the White House was impressed with him:

> "Lansdale was not in favor... during my period, with either the military or with the State Department. He was in the doghouse with both of them. And I was convinced they were wrong. I was convinced he was not a wheeler dealer; he was not an irresponsible swashbuckler; and I finally succeeded in getting him his star as a general–very difficult... he

was the object of some distrust. I thought and still think he was a very able person.... Anyway, he remained active, both in connection with Southeast Asia and Cuba, up until the time I left in January of '64."

Lansdale did not get the ambassadorship; but in April, 1961, his reputation was such that the Kennedy administration's program to "turn around" the Cuban Revolution in the aftermath of the Bay of Pigs was put under his direction. Operation MONGOOSE, which was to become the largest clandestine operation since the Bay of Pigs, was intended to replace the Castro government and included elaborate plans to expedite the operation through Castro's murder.

This examination and policy assessment–initiated in May, 1961–led in November of that year to a final decision to implement Kennedy's new covert program in Cuba. Operation Mongoose was designed to do what the Bay of Pigs invasion failed to do: remove the Communist Castro regime from power in Cuba. Orchestrated by the CIA and Department of Defense under the direction of Edward Lansdale, Operation Mongoose constituted a multiplicity of plans with wide-ranging purpose and scope.

Oversight for the operation was provided by the 5412/2 Special Group, under the auspices of the National Security Council, expanded to include General Maxwell D. Taylor, Attorney General Robert Kennedy, and Brigadier General Lansdale. Boots-on-the-ground level for Mongoose was led by Edward Lansdale at the Defense Department and William King Harvey at the CIA.

The main thrust of Lansdale's plans was a series of large scale "dirty tricks" meant to evoke a call to arms against Cuba in the international community. One plan called for a space launch at Cape Canaveral to be sabotaged and blamed on Cuban agents. OPERATION BINGO called for a staged attack on the US Navy Base at Guantanamo Bay in hopes of creating a mandate for the US military to overthrow Castro.

From March through August 1960, the CIA had plans aimed at undermining Castro and his appeal to the public by sabotaging his speeches. The schemes were aimed at discrediting Castro by influencing his behavior and by changing his appearance. One plan discussed was to spray his broadcast studio with a compound similar to LSD but was scrapped because the compound was too unreliable. Another plot was to lace a box of Castro's cigars with a chemical known to cause temporary disorientation. The CIA's plans to undermine Castro's public image went so far as to line his shoes with thallium salts which would cause his beard to fall out. The plan was to lace his shoes with the salts while he was on a trip outside Cuba. He was expected to leave his shoes outside his hotel room to be polished, at which point the salts would be administered. The plan was abandoned because Castro canceled the trip.

Operation Mongoose was divided into 32 sections, each named for different species of Mongooses. The final component of Mongoose was psychological warfare. Air Force Brigadier General Edward Lansdale hands-on commanded the PsyOps portion of Operation Mongoose. Lansdale created an anti-Castro radio broadcast that covertly aired in Cuba. Leaflets were distributed that depicted Castro as getting fat and wealthy at the expense of citizens. Operatives circulated stories about heroic freedom fighters. The plans varied in efficacy and intention, from propagandistic purposes for effective disruption of the Cuban government and economy. Plans included the use of US Army Special Forces, destruction of Cuban sugar crops, and mining of harbors.

Operation Northwoods was a plan proposed in 1962, which was signed by the Chairman of the Joint Chiefs of Staff and presented to Secretary of Defense Robert McNamara for approval. It intended to use false flag operations to justify intervention in Cuba. Among courses of action considered were real and simulated attacks on US or foreign soil which would be blamed on the Cuban government. These were to involve attacking or reporting fake attacks on Cuban exiles, damaging US bases and ships, so-called "Cuban" aircraft attacking Central American countries such as Haiti or the Dominican Republic, having shipments of arms found on nearby beaches, faking a Cuban military plane destroying an American civilian aircraft, and the possible development of other false-flag terror campaign on US soil. Kennedy rejected the Operation Northwoods operation and never carried out.

At one point, the CIA even enlisted the aid of the Mafia—who were eager to regain their Cuban casino operations—to plot an assassination attempt against Castro; William Harvey was one of the CIA case officers who directly dealt with mafioso John Roselli. According to the CIA documents–the so-called Family Jewels that were declassified in 2007–one assassination attempt on Fidel Castro prior to the Bay of Pigs invasion involved noted American mobsters John Roselli, Sam Giancana and Santo Trafficante. At least some of the CIA assassination attempts on Castro were given the CIA project name ZRRIFLE.

In September, 1960, Momo Salvatore Giancana–a successor of Al Capone's in the Chicago Outfit–and Miami Syndicate leader Santo Trafficante–who were both on the FBI's Ten Most Wanted list at that time–were indirectly contacted by the CIA about the possibility of Fidel Castro›s assassination. Johnny Roselli, a member of the Las Vegas Syndicate, was used to get access to Mafia bosses. The go-between from the CIA was Robert Maheu of the Howard Hughes organization, who introduced himself as a representative of several international businesses in Cuba that Castro expropriated.

On September 14, 1960, Maheu met with Roselli in a New York City hotel and offered him US$ 150,000 for the "removal" of Castro. James O'Connell, who identified himself as Maheu's associate but who actually was the chief of the CIA's operational support division, was present during the meeting. The declassified documents did not reveal if Roselli, Giancana or Trafficante accepted a down payment for the job. According to the CIA files, it was Giancana who suggested poison pills as a means to doctor Castro's food or drinks. Such pills–manufactured by the CIA's Technical Services Division–were given to Giancana's nominee named Juan Orta. Giancana recommended Orta as being an official in the Cuban government, who had access to Castro.

The mafioso was introduced to the CIA by former FBI Agent Robert Mahue. Mahue had known Roselli since the 1950s and was aware of his connection to the gambling syndicate. Under the alias "John Rawlson," Roselli was tasked with recruiting Cubans from Florida to help in the assassination of Castro. Nothing came of the plot, as might be expected in any "Keystone Cops" scenario.

The CIA recruited mob bosses Sam Giancana, Santo Trafficante, and other mobsters, to assassinate Fidel Castro. In April, 1967, the Inspector General issued a report on the various plots conceived to assassinate Fidel Castro. The report separated plots out into several time frames starting with "prior to August 1960" and ending with "Late 1962 until well into 1963". While confirmed, the assassination plots are an "imperfect history", and due to the "sensitivity of the operations being discussed", no official records were kept regarding planning, authorizations, or the implementation of such plots". The Inspector General report detailed "at least three, and perhaps four, schemes that were under consideration" during a time range between March and August 1960. It is speculated that all the schemes considered at this time could have been in the planning process at the same time. The first plan in this time frame involved an attack on the radio station Castro used to "broadcast his speeches with an aerosol spray of a chemical that produced reactions similar to those of LSD [lysergic acid]". Nothing came of this plot, because the chemical could not be relied on to produce the intended effects.

Jake Esterline claimed that a box of cigars–which was treated with chemicals–was also considered in the plot to assassinate Castro. The scheme was that the chemical would produce "temporary personality disorientation"; and having "Castro smoke one before making a speech," would result in Castro making a "public spectacle of himself." Esterline later admitted that even though he could not exactly recall what the cigars were intended to do, he did not believe they were lethal. The lethality of the cigars is contradicted by Sidney Gottlieb who "remembers the scheme… being concerned with killing".

The CIA even tried to embarrass Castro by attempting to sneak thallium salts [a heavy metal poison], a potent depilatory, into Castro's shoes, causing "his beard, eyebrows, and pubic hair, to fall out". The idea for this plan revolved around "destroying Castro's image as 'The Beard'". Unfortunately for the CIA, but fortunately for the dictator, Castro did not make the intended trip, and the scheme fell through".

A 2011 declassified CIA volume titled "Air Operations, March 1960–April 1961" from the comprehensive Official History of the Bay of Pigs Operation, made the indication that "it was clear from the outset that air operations would play a key role in the CIA program to oust the Cuban leader." By the summer of 1960, the JMATE, a unit under the direct command of Richard M. Bissell and the DPD, strove to acquire "aircraft for infiltration, propaganda, and supply drops to dissent groups within Cuba." By July 1960, it became clear that "tactical air operations with combat aircraft would play a major role in JMATE plans."

In August 1960, the CIA initiated the first phase of a plan entitled "Gambling Syndicate". Richard Bissell had CIA contact Robert Maheu pull in Johnny Roselli, a member of the syndicate of Las Vegas. Maheu, disguised as a personal relations executive for a company suffering severe financial losses in Cuba due to Castro›s actions, offered Roselli $150,000 for the successful assassination of Castro. Roselli provided involved a co-conspirator, "Sam Gold", later to be identified as Chicago gangster Sam Giancana and "Joe, the courier", identified later as Santos Trafficante, the Cosa Nostra chieftain of Cuba. Additionally, Dr. Edward Gunn recalled receiving a box of cigars that he was tasked with poisoning; however, the cigars were destroyed by Gunn in 1963.

Several schemes, in regard to the best way to deliver the syndicate poison, that were considered during this time included "(1) something highly toxic... to be administered with a pin... (2) bacterial material in liquid form; (3) bacterial treatment of a cigarette or cigar; and (4) a handkerchief treated with bacteria". According to Bissell, the most viable option presented was bacterial liquids. The final product, however, was solid botulin pills that would dissolve in liquid.

Roselli, along with associate "Sam Gold", used their connection to coerce Cuban official Juan Orta to perform the assassination through his gambling bills. Orta—after being provided several pills of "high lethal content", reportedly attempted the assassination multiple times but eventually pulled out after getting "cold feet".

The plan to assassinate Castro by poison pill was canceled after the Bay of Pigs; Furthermore, the Inspector General's report speculates that this attempt failed because Castro no longer visited the restaurant where the pill was supposed to be administered to him. The second phase of the Gambling Syndicate operation began in May 1961 with Project ZRRIFLE, which was headed by Harvey.

Harvey was responsible for eight assassination attempts on Castro, but none of these attempts were proficient at accomplishing any foreign policy objectives. This section of the assassination scheme program contained "an Executive Action Capability [assassination of foreign leader], a general stand-by capability to carry out assassinations when required". Project ZRRIFLE main purpose was to spot potential agents and research assassination techniques that might be used. Project ZRRIFLE and the agency's operations in Cuba funneled and fumbled their way into the program in November 1961 when Harvey became the head of the task force for Cuba.

As the months of 1962 went by, the Verona mob constructed a team of three men to strike at Castro; however, the plans were canceled twice with the Inspector General's report citing "'conditions inside'... then the October missile crisis threw plans awry". Harvey drew the conclusion about this particular effort that "the three militia never did leave for Cuba". The connections between Roselli and the CIA fell apart once Harvey had been notified that Roselli was on the FBI's watch list. As earnest or wacky or bizarre as all the assassination attempts were, they all smacked of involvement by Edward Lansdale. His name, however, never came up.

Noam Chomsky said that a post missile crises sabotage by the killed "four hundred workers", according to a Cuban government letter to the UN secretary general.However, such direct provocations of the Cubans and Soviets ran at odds with both JFK's Missile Crisis-defusing pledge to remove US Jupiter missiles from Turkey in exchange for the withdrawal of Soviet missiles from Cuba and efforts made towards rapprochement with Castro in the aftermath of the crisis. The missile swap had been seen by many as an even trade that saved face for both sides when considering the capabilities of each to deliver a serious strike to the other. Kennedy subsequently sought dialogue with Castro to reverse the two nations' acrimonious relationship. As a result of the CIA's continued defiance, however, tensions between the CIA and Cuba and between the President and the Agency, festering since the failed Bay of Pigs invasion, continued to escalate.

In early 1963, The CIA learned that Castro loved diving. The CIA decided to create an infected diving suit that would kill Castro slowly, over a long period of time, by lining the suit with tuberculosis and "contaminating the breathing apparatus with tubercle bacilli". The infected diving suit did not succeed. The plan was betrayed, and Castro learned of the attempt.

Various other methods of assassination thought of by the CIA after the missile crisis the last apprehended on a rooftop within rifle range of Castro, at the end of February or beginning of March 1963 included exploding seashells, having a former lover slip him poison pills in cold cream, and exposing him to various other poisoned items such as a fountain pen.

Another attempt at Castro's life was by way of a fountain pen loaded with the poison Black Leaf 40 and passed to a Cuban asset in Paris the day of President Kennedy's assassination, November 22, 1963, and even ice cream. There were also plans to assassinate Castro and one to eliminate Rolando Cubela, a Cuban revolutionary hero. The plot for Cubela began as an operation to recruit someone close to Castro to launch a coup.

The US Senate's Church Committee of 1975 stated that it had confirmed at least eight separate CIA run plots to assassinate Castro. Fabian Escalante–who was long tasked with protecting the life of Castro–contends that there have been 638 separate CIA assassination schemes or attempts on Castro's life. Plans included mafia-style execution endeavors, among others. There were plans to blow up Castro during his visit to Ernest Hemingway's museum in Cuba.

The last documented attempt on Castro's life was in 2000 and involved placing 90 kg of explosives under a podium in Panama where he would give a talk. Castro's personal security team discovered the explosives before he arrived. The CIA in 1962 considered a plan called "Operation Bounty", which would have involved dropping leaflets over Cuba offering financial rewards to the Cuban population for the assassination of various individuals, including $5,000 to $20,000 for informants, $57,000 for department heads, $97,000 for foreign Communists operating in Cuba, up to $1 million for members of the Cuban government, and only $0.02 for Castro himself, which was meant "to denigrate" him in the eyes of the Cuban people. The top-secret document which revealed the plan was never put into practice. Lansdale's name was never mentioned in the committee report. He retired in 1968 and died February 23, 1987.

A key form of documentation used to construct the timeline of plots was oral testimony collected years after the plots were originally planned. Like most covert operations—especially those hatched by Edward Lansdale–the plan to oust the Cuban dictator was an uneven and slippery thing. Who was paid to do what, with what, and to whom, is still not clear, and probably never will be. But one thing is certain: Robert Kennedy was in charge at the government level. Convinced he hypocritically indicated that he—the president–had been betrayed by his military and intelligence advisors in the decision to launch the Bay of Pigs invasion, John Kennedy placed Cuba in the hands of the one man he knew he could trust. But what could be done? At a White House meeting in November, 1961, RFK scribbled the following in his notes:

"My idea is to stir things up on the island with espionage, sabotage, general disorder, run and operated by Cubans themselves with every group but Batistaites and Communists. Do not know if we will be successful in overthrowing Castro but we have nothing to lose in my estimate." [italics by the present author]

The game of espionage–small, covert, special, operations–not another large-scale military invasion–would be the method this time, coming from the fertile mind of Edward Lansdale. Kennedy's terms of art was "counterinsurgency," and "social reform under pressure." Both were calculated euphemisms in line with the hypocrisy of the Kennedy administration. Robert "Bobbie" Kennedy was so enamored of the fearless commandos and real-life James Bonds who did such work that he once invited Special Forces troops to Hickory Hill to instruct his children on how to swing from trees.

Lansdale outlined the coordinated program of political, psychological, military, sabotage, and intelligence, operations, as well as proposed assassination attempts on key political leaders, including Castro—much the same as had been the case when, On April 17, 1961, 1,400 Cuban exiles launched what became a botched invasion at the Bay of Pigs on the south coast of Cuba. There remained grave concern to the United States given Cuba's geographical proximity to the United States and brought Cuba into play as a new and significant factor in the Cold War. Lansdale's expertise was again called to the fore.

## The Aftermath:

The disaster at the Bay of Pigs had a lasting impact on the Kennedy administration. Determined to make up for the failed invasion, the administration initiated Operation Mongoose—a plan to sabotage and destabilize the Cuban government and economy, which included the possibility of assassinating Castro. That operation also failed to topple Castro.

A congressional investigation of the CIA later uncovered eight separate plots of varying levels of absurdity between 1960 and 1965. The Kennedys knew the meaning of the term "plausible deniability" all too well and had been taught the old Boston Irish political rule, "never write it down."

"Get rid of Castro and the Castro regime, quote-unquote," is how Sam Halpern–executive officer of the CIA team charged with carrying out Operation Mongoose–described his orders from Director Helms.

"And when I asked Dick, what does 'Get rid of' mean, he said, 'Sam, use your imagination.' That was it... Now what does that mean? throw him in the ashcan? Kill him? or what? And nobody could tell me. Just get rid of. Remove him from power basically. Helms himself was responding to relentless pressure from the White House. 'You haven't lived until you've had Bobby Kennedy rampant on your back,'" Helms said.

Decades after the incidents, a declassified report by Inspector General Lyman Kirkpatrick detailed the history of the operation...

"The CIA's budget estimation for this covert operation was approximately $4.4 million. The paper signed by Eisenhower was also the sole report issued by the government throughout the entire project. The report highlights the US Government's secrecy—its insistence on plausible deniability. America, and especially John F. Kennedy, did not increase its reputation for integrity by the operations or the report.

According to the after-action report, other agencies were brought in to assist with the planning and execution of Operation Mongoose. "There was a considerable degree of cooperation between the CIA and other of the concerned agencies: the Department of Defense, the Department of State, the Federal Bureau of Investigation, Immigration and Naturalization Service, and others.... As the operation's leader, Brigadier General Lansdale received briefings and updates from these agencies and reported directly to a group of high-ranking government officials, known as Special Group-Augmented (SG-A)... As was common throughout the Kennedy presidency, decision making would be centralized and housed within the secret Special Group (SG-A). At this time, Operation Mongoose was underway."

By the 50th anniversary of the Bay of Pigs Invasion, it was known that the CIA task force in charge of the paramilitary assault knew the operation could not succeed without becoming an open invasion supported by the US military. According to Peter Kornbluh, this was the most important revelation of the declassification of the official history of the CIA…

The CIA's Official History of the Bay of Pigs Operation notes that limited air cover left the Brigade air force open to attacks by Castro's forces. Both Kennedys ignored the fact that limited air strikes would prevent the Brigade air force from being effective because of the risk of counterattack by the Cuban air force. The Official History notes that the use of napalm had not been officially approved until the next day, April 18, 1961. 10 days later TIDE dropped 5 B-26 bombs.

As for blame: A commission led by General Maxwell Taylor, known as the Taylor Committee, investigated the failures of the Bay of Pigs invasion. The objective was to find out who was responsible for the disaster. In one of his volumes of an internal report written between 1974-1984, CIA Chief Historian Jack Pfeiffer criticized the Taylor Committee's investigation because it held the CIA primarily responsible for the Bay of Pigs fiasco. At the end of the fourth volume, Pfeiffer lamented that Taylor had a hand in perpetuating the idea that "President Kennedy was a white knight misled by overconfident, if not mischievous, CIA activists. Bobby's biographer Evan Thomas said, "People still see the CIA as this sinister, nefarious force. It was a fundamentally foolish thing to do, and Bobby bears real responsibility for it."

Samuel Halpern–a CIA co-organizer–conveyed the breadth of involvement: "CIA and the US Army and military forces and Department of Commerce, and Immigration, Treasury, God knows who else–everybody was in Mongoose." Lansdale criticized the CIA effort to ramp up their activities to meet Operation Mongoose's expedient timelines. Robert McCone of the CIA complained that Lansdale's timeline was too accelerated and that it would be difficult to achieve the tasks demanded in such a short timeframe.

Director McCone criticized the handling of the operation, believing that "national policy was too cautious" and suggested a US military effort to train more guerrillas—a two-edged sword of criticism of Lansdale.

Lansdale's reply was to recommend a more aggressive short-term plan of action. He believed that time was of the essence, especially given intensified Soviet military build-up in Cuba. New plans were drawn to recruit more Cubans to infiltrate the Castro regime, to interrupt Cuban radio and television broadcasts, and to deploy commando sabotage units.

Inspector General Kirkpatrick's report went on to say… "During the planning of "OPERATION MONGOOSE" a March, 1962 CIA Memorandum sought a brief, but precise description of pretexts which the Joint Chiefs of Staff considered would provide justification for American military intervention in Cuba… There was a meeting of the Special Group (Augmented) in Secretary of State David Rusk's conference room on August 10, 1962 at which Secretary of Defense Robert McNamara broached the subject of the liquidation of Cuban leaders. The discussion resulted in a Project MONGOOSE action memorandum prepared by Edwards Landsdale.

The formerly classified memorandum depicted the way in which the CIA and the Joint Chiefs of Staff sought a reason to invade the island of Cuba that would be acceptable to the American people. The document states, 'such a plan would enable a logical build-up of incidents to be combined with other seemingly unrelated events to camouflage the ultimate objective and create the necessary impression of Cuban rashness and irresponsibility on a large scale, directed at other countries as well as the United States… The desired resultant from the execution of this plan would be to place the United States in the apparent position of suffering defensible grievances from a rash and irresponsible government of Cuba and to develop an international image of a Cuban threat to peace in the Western Hemisphere… Another significant consideration was that any U.S. military intervention in Cuba should not involve the Soviet Union…"

The most significant outcome of The Cuban Project were the events leading up to the Cuban Missile Crisis of 1962. That was the nearest the world ever came to the start of World War III. That issue is discussed elsewhere in this book.

Operation Mongoose was suspended on October 30, 1962, but 3 of 10 six-man sabotage teams had already been deployed to Cuba. Historian

Stephen Rabewrote that reports from the US Senate Church Committee reveal that from June, 1963 onward—after the missile crisis–the Kennedy administration intensified its war against Cuba. Noam Chomsky argued that "terrorist operations continued through the tensest moments of the missile crisis", remarking that "they were formally canceled on October 30, several days after the Kennedy and Khrushchev agreement, but went on nonetheless".

The CIA integrated propaganda, "economic denial, and sabotage to attack the Cuban state as well as specific targets within" One example cited is an incident where CIA agents, seeking to assassinate Castro, provided a Cuban official, Rolando Cubela Secades, with a ballpoint pen rigged with a poisonous hypodermic needle. During this post missile crisis period, the CIA received authorization for 13 major operations in Cuba, including attacks on an electric power plant, an oil refinery, and a sugar mill.

Rabe argued that the "Kennedy administration... showed no interest in Castro's repeated request that the United States cease its campaign of sabotage and terrorism against Cuba. Kennedy did not pursue a dual-track policy toward Cuba... The United States would entertain only proposals of surrender." Rabe further documented that "Exile groups, such as Alpha 66 and the Second Front of Escambray, staged hit-and-run raids on the island... on ships transporting goods... purchased arms in the United States and launched... attacks from the Bahamas."

According to Top Secret transcripts declassified in 2021, Scott Breckinridge–in his 1975 Church Committee hearing–told senators that the CIA had also contemplated using botulinum toxin to lace cigars to be delivered to Castro, but this plan never went forward.

Harvard Historian Jorge Domínguez stated that the CIA's scope included sabotage actions against a railway bridge, a saw mill, petroleum storage facilities, a molasses storage container, a petroleum refinery, a power plant, a sawmill, and a floating crane, to undermine the Cuban economy. The Executive Committee of the National Security Council recommended various courses of action, "including 'using selected Cuban exiles to sabotage key Cuban installations in such a manner that the action could plausibly be attributed to Cubans in Cuba as well as sabotaging Cuban cargo and shipping, and [Soviet] Bloc cargo and shipping to Cuba."

Edward Lansdale's awards, decorations, and medals:

Among Lansdale's decorations were the Distinguished Service Medal awarded by the Air Force for his work in Indo-China during the period 1954-1956, the National Security Medal awarded by the National Security Council for his service in the Philippines during the period 1950- 1953, the Philippine's Legion of Honor, and the Philippine's Medal of Military Merit.

Many of Lansdale's private papers and effects were destroyed in a fire at his McLean home in 1972. In 1981, Lansdale donated most of his remaining papers to Stanford University's Hoover Institution. Edward Lansdale died of a heart ailment on February 23, 1987 and was buried in Arlington National Cemetery.

Lansdale was considered by some—like the present author—to be a hero, despite the violence his leadership and his direct action caused. He was—for some—the genius cowboy who sometimes skirts the rules to achieve the just goals of Western democracy; for others, the embodiment of an arrogant foreign policy gone dangerously wrong. I have no real argument with that sentiment except that the man stood up to powerful people with whom he disagreed and paid the price. He acted as a loyal American soldier and intelligence agent while still upholding his principles of democracy and just treatment for the unjustly treated lower class of people all over the world where he served. He did so in the face of strong opposition by the leaders of those countries and of such well-known leaders as Defense Secretary McNamara, the American ambassador to the Philippines, JUSMAG chief Major Albert Pierson, and famed generals Curtis LeMay and Victor Krulak.

A Soviet hero came to the fore. Vasily Aleksandrovich Arkhipov **[January 30, 1926-August 19, 1998] was a Soviet Naval officer who prevented a Soviet nuclear torpedo launch during the Cuban Missile Crisis.** Scarcely anyone in the world is aware of the unsung story of Soviet naval officer Vasili Arkhipov—the Brigade Chief of Staff on submarine B-59—who refused to fire a nuclear missile and thereby helped to save the world from World War III and nuclear disaster. Then, on October 24, two days after Kennedy announced the quarantine, there was a glimmer of hope: Sigint confirmed that at least one Soviet ship headed toward

Cuba had stopped and changed direction and appeared to be rerouting back toward the Soviet Union—a sign the Soviets were not intending to challenge Kennedy's quarantine. Yet it was also crucial that American officials feel confident in that assessment. This close to the ledge, there was simply no room for miscalculation.

The crisis was over; but the naval quarantine continued until the Soviets agreed to remove their IL–28 bombers from Cuba, and—per agreement, on November 20, 1962–the United States ended its quarantine. US Jupiter missiles were removed from Turkey in April, 1963.

*NY Times* reporter Scali described what Khrushchev told him when Scali asked him why he really backed down.

"Khruschev said to me, 'The US is a funny country. It will endure a long period of insults, minor attacks inflicted upon it, and a whole host of threats. Then it will shoot you in the heart.'"

## Saving Beta Israel, 1984-2022:

Have you ever been bullied, put down, discriminated against, or a victim of inequality? If so, I am concerned for you. If all of that happened for many years, I sorrow for you. If you became desperate, and no help was in sight, then I pity and am angry for you. You need a big brother, and you need him now. The following is that kind of story–the saving of Beta Israel.

## Background:

On the basis of the available evidence, it does not appear likely that the earliest Jews entered Ethiopia in single united group. It seems far more plausible that they arrived in the country in small groups alongside other non-Jewish merchants, settlers, soldiers, and nomads. In addition, other Judaized elements probably entered Ethiopia from Arabia at any time from the 1st to the 6th century CE. Jewish practices are widespread throughout the Horn of Africa indicating that the Jewish immigrants did not live in isolation from their neighbors.

A wealth of historical and genealogical evidence exists to show that the Beta Israel originated from Jews who migrated from Kush to Aksum sometime between the first and fourth century CE. Judaism entered

Aksum prior to the establishment of the Christian Church there. This Jewish community that was exiled from Aksum to the Semien and Tana areas in the 6th century by King Kaleb ultimately produced the Beta Israel society.

Beta Israel Jews have historically inhabited the northwestern area of the Ethiopian highlands and the western portion of what is today Northern Sudan. Because historically, they were prohibited from owning land by Abyssinian law, the Beta Israel primarily worked as tenant farmers and artisans, blacksmiths, and became excellent ceramicists and potters. Long ago, they spoke a range of Ge'az dialects; but by the 20th century Tiginya and Amharic became the dominant languages which distinguished them from the dominant Abyssinians. The Beta Israel preferred and persisted in being isolated and distinct. As a result, trade was limited; and intermarriage was forbidden by Beta Israel law.

History wrought significant changes; so, an abbreviated timeline will be given:

- The Beta Israel traditionally attributed their descent from the Israelite tribe of Dan. Rabbinic tradition holds that the details and interpretation of the Torah [Written Law] called the Oral Torah or Oral Law, i.e. the unwritten tradition coming directly from Moses on Mount Sinai were part of Beta Israel doctrine and practice. All the laws in the Written Torah are recorded only as part of a narrative describing God imparting this laws and commanding Moses to transmit them to the Jewish nation. Biblical passages—in addition to a number of extra-Biblical traditions—tell of an Israelite presence in Kush, e.g. Zephaniah 3:10, "From beyond the rivers of Cush [Kush] my worshipers, my scattered people, will bring me offerings."

  The history of Ethiopian Jewry goes back millennia. For almost 2,000 years, the Beta Israel had their own community—even their own kingdom and army—in the Simien Mountains. While the Beta Israel were isolated away from the rest of Jewry, they came to believe that they were among the only Jews left on earth after the Temple's destruction. Slowly, word of their existence filtered out to the rest of the world. Marco Polo and

Benjamin of Tudela wrote of the existence of an independent Jewish nation—"a Mosaic kingdom lying on the other side of the rivers of Ethiopia."

The community feared that Jewish traditions and learning were in danger of being forgotten; so, they made an effort to gather knowledge from the Jewish centers of Palestine and Babylonia. That resulted in the creation of two works of the Talmud. There was at the time also several antagonistic factions—the Pharisees, Sadducces, and Zealots, as well as several small isolated sects.

- 6th century CE—The earliest Christian emperors appeared not to have either the mandate nor the religious zeal to pursue a policy of extermination of the Jewish people. However, in the 6th century CE, Ethiopian emperor Kaleb—a fervent king of Aksum—became known for widescale conversions, church building, and a harsh anti-pagan campaign. He lumped Jews with the pagans. His relationship with Aksum's Jews was described euphemistically as "restless". He overthrew a Jewish king in South Arabia in favor of a Christian and extended his actions to include the Aksum's Jewish population shortly thereafter. Beta Israel further isolated itself as a protective measure, and their place in Ethiopia became known as "the country to which the King of the Aksumites exiles anyone whom he has sentenced to be banished."

- 9th century CE—A Jewish scholar identified himself as a Danite and a citizen of a "Jewish state beyond the rivers of Cush, i.e. the Beta Israel were Jews specifically from the tribe of Dan.

- 12th-14th centuries CE—a traveler referred in his writings to a tribe of Israelites in Nubia—the medieval name for the Nile Valley region of Kush in northern Sudan. Also–an originally pagan community which later and for most of its known history—became Christian, the Zagwe, had traditions suggesting that their dynasty was initiated by Beta Israel—Jews. The Zagwe claimed to have descended from Moses and Zipporah.

- 1270 CE—The year marks a major turning point in Ethiopian history. It was the year during which a new dynasty traced its descent and right to power from King Solomon. They consolidated their power over the Christian areas of Ethiopia and set about pursuing their hegemony of the independent powers of the Ethiopian highlands.
- 1314-1344 CE—After the reign of King Amda Siyon, almost all Ethiopian kings were committed to the political subjugation of the Judaized population in the regions of Semien, Woggara, and Dambiya. The Jews were injured both physically and economically during the era's battles. Siyon's grandson threatened the Jews with loss of their land rights if they failed to convert to Christianity. Isolation of the Jews and intentionally close proximity to bigoted Christians led the Beta Israel to abandon many traditional customs over time.
- 1434-1468 CE—Fighting and hiding led the Jews to sacrifice their lives and to adopt a monastic status unique to Jewish history. Maintenance of certain Jewish customs required greater monetary cost than others; the impoverished Beta Israel gradually gave the costly ones up. The Christians developed a policy of regarding Beta Israel as heresy. The sacrifices from battles and military invasions led to the loss of textual content and their numbers dwindled.
- 14-15th centuries CE—Christian kings required forced conversions and hardened the isolated "different" status of the Jews. They were exposed to Christian missionaries and Christian monasticism. It became evermore difficult to maintain a distinct Jewish quality among the Beta Israelites.
- 15th century CE—Ethiopian emperor Fasilide ordered the expulsion of Portuguese Christian armies and restored the Ethiopian Orthodox Church. He created a revival and a period of tolerance that benefitted Beta Israel since the revival included religious tolerance and permitted open trade of Ethiopian spices. The Beta Israel formally adopted the model of Christian monasticism. That resulted in changes in Beta Israel literature,

customs, prayers, arts, introduction of roving sages, and segregation of the sexes as practiced by the Christians.

- 1607-1632 CE—Hostilities between the Christian Abyssinian Ethiopians and the Beta Israel resulting in a severe defeat of the Jews. That ended Beta Israel independence. From 1626 on, Beta Israel went into an economic and military downward spiral. The mountain ridge occupied by the Jews was conquered.
- 16th century CE—Hebrew began to disappear as a ritual language and completely vanished with the opening of the 17th century. It was replaced by Ge'ez. The script used in all Ethiopian languages changed over to the Habesha Script.
- Mid-19th century CE—Although the Beta Israel community remained isolated and self-contained, most of the people possessed only a rudimentary of the Jewish symbols and rituals of their religious traditions.
- Early 20th century CE—Jacques Faitlovitch arrived in Ethiopia, and that marked yet another turning point for Beta Israel. He was only the second practicing European Jew to visit the community, and he and his followers slowly introduced Beta Israel back into mainstream Jewish history.
- 1973-1974 CE—Most 20th century poskim [legal religious scholars] looked down upon the Beta Israelis with serious skepticism. The Israeli interior minister of the time issued deportation orders for those living in Israel. However, that was put on hold when a revered scholar and historian insisted that they were truly Jews in every sense of the word. He was so influential, that his influence paved the way for the new Jewish Aliyah—Heb. Ascent, or going up, i.e. traveling up to Israel, one of the most basic tenets of Zionism.

## Timeline of Jewish Aliyah:

- 1862—A Jewish monk led thousands of Jews to Ethiopia via the Red Sea, believing that God would perform a miracle like that of opening of the Red Sea on the journey out of Egypt. This venture ended in tragedy. Many of them died of starvation and epidemic disease before crossing the Ethiopian border. The results if the failed effort made aliya to Jerusalem seem impossible and there was a general sense of despair about repeating the effort.

- 1864—A major German Rabbi—Aziel Hildenheimer—published a call to action wherein he unequivocally recognized the Judaism of Beta Israel and determined that the obligation to save them comprised Arut Israel—a Jewish mutual responsibility.

- Mid-19th century—The population of Beta Israel was estimated at 250,000, but the number was greatly reduced by the famine of 1881-1882. In 1908, in response to Hildenheimer's pleas, the chief rabbis of 45 countries came out with a unified statement officially declaring that Ethiopian Jews were indeed Jewish. That designation led to open support among the majority of European Jews and fostered the desire for aliya for them.

- 1973—the modern era of aliya missions by the heroes of this book led up to the current day. From 1973, the Beta Israel community languished under the dictatorship of Lt. Col. Mengistu Haile Mariam. In the early 1980s, Mengistu forbade the Jews to leave, and many had to cross into Sudan illegally on foot. Israel intervened, and 7,000 were covertly flown from Sudan to Israel. By 1984, 8,000 members of the community were given permission and moved to Israel quasi-legally. In 1985, Sudan caved-in to pressure by its neighboring Muslim states and halted emigration. Large numbers of Ethiopian Jews were stranded in Sudan as a result.

Several months later, the United States flew 500 of them to Israel in Operation Joshua. After prolonged negotiations and huge bribes, Israel and Mengistu reached an agreement again allowing Jewish emigration.

The history of Israel's secret missions to save Ethiopian Beta Israel: Operations Moses/Brothers, Joshua/Sheba, and Solomon:

## Operation Moses/Brothers, 1984-1985—

Operation Moses was the covert evacuation of Ethiopian Jews from Sudan by a cooperative union of Israeli Mossad, the United States CIA through its embassy in Khartoum, mercenaries, and well-paid Sudanese security forces. The Mossad covertly rescued Jewish-Ethiopian refugees who suffered from persecution in Sudan by smuggling them all the way to safety in Israel, using a base at the once-abandoned holiday resort of Arous Village on the Sudanese Red Sea coast. After a secret Israeli cabinet meeting in November, 1984, the decision was made to go forward with Moses. It involved air transport by TEA [Trans European Airways] of Ethiopian Jews from Sudan via Brussels to Israel, ending January 5, 1985

Over the seven weeks of the mission, ~8,000 Ethiopian Jews escaped to Israel on more than 30 flights. The operation took place during Ethiopia's worst-ever drought and famine—which killed more than 400,000 people. As the images of starving children reached the West, many people made an effort to help. We are the World—written by Michael Jackson and Lionel Richie—featured more than 40 American pop stars. It became the biggest single charity song of all time and raised more than $63 million.

"It was the only time when Europeans had extracted Africans from the continent, not to be enslaved, but to be freed."

–Gad Shimron, Mossad agent involved in Operation Moses.

In the original Operation Moses, the refugees were met by Israeli Navy Seals who brought them to a ship, which then sailed away with little difficulty. In 1977, roughly 7,000 Jews became homeless and 12,000 made a perilous walking journey from the northern mountains of Ethiopia to the border of Sudan during a vicious civil war. Along the way, they endured hunger, thirst, attacks by bandits, and predation by wild beasts. ~4,000 died on the trek. Many thousands of others, including a great many children died in refugee camps along the way. Israel was the only country to actually do something and was successful in transporting thousands out of the hellhole of hostile Sudan and Ethiopia to safety in the Jewish homeland. Many parents brought the bodies of the dead children on the aircraft with them; so, they could be buried in Israel. That came to an end when worldwide publicity brought it to light and humiliated Sudan and its neighbors. The mission was not complete, however.

Operation Brothers was then instituted under the aegis of the Mossad. Gad Shimron and his fellow agents sought and obtained funding to purchase the resort and to refurbish it as a fully operational international tourist scuba diving vacation location. The resourceful agents created a shell company under the aegis of lending institutions in Switzerland. It was so successful that the Sudanese government and its security agents were never suspicious. In fact, it turned a profit for the Israeli government after expenses.

The way the operation worked was ingenious. Genuine tourists were received and treated like class with good lodgings, food, and diving experiences. The refugees always came at night and never encountered the tourists who were mainly from Germany. It the darkest hours of the night, the refugees silently boarded ships and were taken to a final destination in Israel—~200 at a time.

At one point, four members of Shimron's team—including the operation's commander—were surrounded by a group of 20 armed Sudanese soldiers. The soldiers stopped them on a beach just as they were about to load a group of refugees into a waiting boat which was to take them to a larger ship sitting in deep international water off shore.

"For a second," Shimron said when following behind the group, "I thought we were finished."

He saw one of his fellow agents lowering his hands and arguing with the Sudanese soldiers. He was yelling at the officer for shooting at poor defenseless European tourists who had paid good money to the resort and the government for a night-dive. The Sudanese—who had never seen nor heard of tourists or of diving—were confused, and they folded without further tension.

It was too close a call to ignore. Shimron and his team stopped evacuating people by boats and switched to Hercules cargo planes for their evacuations.

That required some gentle persuasion of the refugees by the Mossad agents.

"You have to understand what it was like for many of the Ethiopian refugees who had never seen a plane in their lives before. For them, it was like Jonah and the Whale," Shimron said.

In all, ~6,000 Ethiopians were rescued during Operation Brothers. The enormity of what they had done hit Shimron "when visiting the absorption center in Israel where the refugees had been placed. There was a small child—maybe seven or eight-years old. He came up to me, tugged on my sleeve, and said, 'Uncle, I remember you from the red truck.' I'll admit, I'm not the sentimental type, but I may have shed a few tears," Shimron said.

However, the Mossad agents estimated that ~1,000 were left behind, and there were more than 1,000 "orphans of circumstance" left without parents upon arrival in Israel.

**Operation Joshua/Sheba—**

All 100 US Senators signed a secret petition to President Ronald Reagan asking him to have the evacuation of Beta Israel resume. Vice President George H.W. Bush arranged for Operation Joshua to commence on March 22, 1985. 6 USAF C-130 Hercules transport aircraft were dispatched, landing near Al Qadarif, Sudan. It was a multi-cultural area, and none too friendly towards Jews or Americans. 650 Jews were brought in from the camps and flown to Ovida Airport in Southern Israel.

**Operation Solomon—**

In 1991, Beta Israel's situation again became desperate during the Second Sudanese Civil War of 1983 to 2005 between the central Sudanese government and the Sudan People's Liberation Army. Roughly two million people died as a result of war, famine, and disease, caused by the conflict. Four million people in southern Sudan were displaced at least once–and often repeatedly–during the war. The civilian death toll is one of the highest of any war since World War II and was marked by a large number of human rights violations, including slavery and mass killings. Serious shortages of fuel and bread caused widespread rioting. On June 30, 1989, military officers replaced the civilian government. With a heavy Muslim influence, in March, 1991, a new penal code–the Criminal Act of 1991–instituted harsh punishments nationwide, including amputations and stoning. Again, Jews did not fare well.

It is estimated that 200,000 Southern Sudanese and Nuba children and women were taken into slavery—mainly to North Sudan—during raids perpetrated in Southern Sudanese towns and villages. On the pretext of fighting Southern Sudanese rebels, the National Islamic government of the Sudan (GOS) deployed its regular armed forces and militia notoriously known as the People's Defense Forces (PDF) to attack and raid villages in the South and the Nuba Mountains for slaves and cattle.

Osama bin Laden and his Al Qaeda organization moved to Sudan in 1991. Osama brought some wealth to Sudan while he directed some of his first terrorist attacks out of Sudan. In 1990-1991, the Sudanese government supported Saddam Hussein in the Gulf War. This changed American attitudes toward the country. Bill Clinton's administration prohibited American investment in the country and supplied money to neighboring countries to repel Sudanese incursions. The US also began attempts to isolate Sudan and began referring to it as a rogue state. That worsened the economy and the lot of the Beta Israelis caught in the cross-fire.

The civil war displaced more than 4 million southerners. Those people were unable to grow food or earn money to feed themselves, and malnutrition and starvation became widespread. Approximately 500,000 Sudanese fled the country.

In the face of an existential threat to its fellow Jews–when rebels seized Addis Abba–the Israeli government set up an emergency plan called, Operation Solomon, and dispatched 34 planes to the Sudan. The planes had their seats removed to make room. One Boeing 747 set a record by transporting out 1,087 passengers in a single flight. Over 36 hours, 14,324 Beta Israelis made it to Israel, safety, and security. It cost Israel $26 million to pay off the dictator led Sudanese government.

## Operation Djibouti Aliyah—

In the summer of 1986, an older man visited villages in the Gondar district of Ethiopia looking for young Jews—both male and female—even younger than the bar-mitzvah age of 13—to take part in a secret operation. His goal was clear: to get to Israel. He explained to parents about the planned route: start on foot to neighboring Djibouti where-once their papers were arranged—they will be flown to Paris and from there to Israel. Simple. The Ethiopians and the Mossad knew there was no other way. A route through Sudan that had been used to smuggle out Ethiopian Jews in Operation Moses had been discovered some time before. During that secret operation—about a year earlier—some 8,000 Jews were brought to Israel, he told them; and an additional 15,000 or more would be airlifted during Operation Solomon in 1991. But now—in mid-1986—the Mossad needed to find a new clandestine route. The first group of young people would be the vanguard force that would launch it.

The older man—a Mossad agent, known only as Z—had a wealth of experience in getting Ethiopian Jews to Israel, particularly via Sudan. The plan he presented to the families helped him to collect a group of 27 people who would embark on a course that would greatly change their lives, he asserted.

In the end, only 23 of them reached Israel. But the ordeals they underwent along the way: brutal violence, sexual abuse, abandonment in foreign prisons in some cases, left them scarred to the present day. The operation acquired heightened secrecy to the point that only a very few people in Israel's defense establishment and the political hierarchy were involved or informed. Not even the Foreign Ministry knew about it.

The operation with so much promise quickly slid from promise to abject failure—the only Mossad operation on behalf of Beta Israel to fail. As the details of the operation began to unfold, it became ever more ensnarled until finally, it was decided not to make any further attempts to bring Ethiopian Jews to Israel via the Djibouti route.

The Djibouti group was actually three separate small groups, which set out from Gondar at intervals of a few weeks. The first one consisted of seven people, two of them women. One of those women was Yeshiwork Dawit, who was 13 at the beginning of her walk. She was one of eight siblings. Her mother urged her to embark on the odyssey, despite her age.

"It was explained to me that the route was supposed to be easy and last four days; first to the city of Wollo, then the city of Kombolcha, from there by bus into Djibouti, and afterward, by plane to Paris, and from Paris to Israel…" Easy.

The group reached Wollo—a province of northeastern Ethiopia— relatively quickly on foot and were housed there under the guise of a group of tourists. Then, they waited. And waited. A guide who had been recruited by the Mossad and was supposed to meet them, did not. They waited for three months, during which they began to arouse the suspicion of local residents. Four of them subsequently left and returned to their home villages. Three remained, Dawit among them.

"We were told that he would accompany us until we met with another man, who would accompany us in Djibouti," Dawit remembered.

The guide eventually arrived; he was from a large, well-known tribe of nomads living in the Ethiopia-Djibouti border region and was very knowledgeable about the area.

"We were told that he would accompany us until we met with another man, who would accompany us in Djibouti."

They were on the road—crossing large desert expanses in broiling-hot August weather for about a week, forced to cope with thirst, illness, encounters with dangerous animals, and robbers. At the end of the route lay the sea, the port of Djibouti.

"Next to the ships someone was waiting especially for our group. He took us to a hut with mattresses, and that was the first night we could rest."

It was also the first night 13-year-old Dawit was raped.

"The guide accompanying us had held back until then. But in the night when we slept together in the hut, he did it. I screamed and cried; and in the morning, I told the man who had met us in the port that if he did not separate me from the guide, I would commit suicide."

Yeshiwork and the two other men from the original group were moved to a spacious house on the outskirts of Djibouti City, the capital. In the villa, she met an older man from Ethiopia who said he had come from Israel to organize pass ports for them.

"But if you get caught, heaven forbid, I don't know you, and you don't know me."

He added, partly as an order, partly as a warning, "Under no circumstances are you to mention the word, "Israel", and whoever gets caught dies alone."

It was a warning Yeshiwork Dawit was to hear many times. Another period of waiting began, this time for the other groups from Ethiopia.

Mamo Biro was in his teens when he joined one of the two remaining groups in Ethiopia. He does not know his exact age, no one does. At the time of this writing, he estimates that he is about fifty. Mamo was born in a small village in the Gondar district, one of 12 siblings. Until sometime in his mid-teens, he helped his parents herd sheep; and he was forcibly recruited, i.e. kidnapped, into the army during the regime of Mengistu Haile Mariam. He kept the fact that he was Jewish, a secret, even from his army friends.

One day Mamo received a letter from his parents, telling him about neighbors who were embarking on a journey to Jerusalem. The letter fired him with a powerful desire to join them. He deserted from the army and returned home. Shortly afterward, Z arrived in the village; the family already knew who he was.

"Z" would get money and pay for the bus tickets and for food. It was known that some people—all males—had already succeeded in reaching Jerusalem."

–Mamo Biro

So, Biro joined Operation Djibouti in August, 1986. His group numbered eight young people, all males, who ranged in age between 13-20. Three guides accompanied them.

"The whole journey was organized by people who—I later learned—worked for the Mossad. They went to Addis Ababa and every time came back with money and arranged for guides."

Like Yeshiwork Dawit's group, the trek took place under grim conditions. And the heat and thirst were the easy part. On the road to Djibouti, they were joined by a non-Jewish family—a mother, a father, and a daughter, age 12. Biro recalled them and could never talk about them without crying.

The three guides beat the father on his head, raped the defenseless mother in front of their innocent daughter then raped the daughter as well.

"I went to people to try to help me erase the memories, but I could not get it out of my head."

Mamo spent years with therapists in Israel to find help, but the memories continued to haunt him. He told Mossad debriefers that the guides ran off when the girl screamed for help. He was afraid to come to her aid fearing retribution from the guide. He remembered vividly how he pretended to be asleep, and she crawled under his long clothes and clung to him, hoping the three monsters would not find her. But, she was wrong. The three returned, found and seized her, and brutalized her all through that horrible night.

"I don't know what happened to them. It could have been that in the end, they killed them."

Not long afterward, they arrived at the house in Djibouti, where they met Yeshiwork Dawit and her friends and also the members of the third and last group.

"Altogether, there were 23 of us in the house. Afterward, two people showed up—whom, today, I can say were Mossad men—one local and one from Israel. One of them knew I had been in the army, and so, he appointed me commander of the group. I would be the person who would get money from him. He showed me how to cover my tracks; so as, not to reveal the villa's location. He taught me how to behave; so, I would not arouse suspicion."

The cover story was that they had come from Ethiopia to look for work. They remained in the villa for many weeks waiting for more people to join them. One of the Mossad agents came by every few days to bring them money. One day, they all went together to have their photographs taken for passports; but they never got to use them. Their prolonged presence in the villa had made the neighbors suspicious, and one morning, they were awakened by loud knocking. They tried to hide but were all caught and herded by local police into a van and delivered to the city jail.

It was a period that came after long years of the "Red Terror", with a great many victims, wars with Eritrea, and a series of recurrent internal wars, decline of Soviet support on the one hand and feeble Western support on the other; and on top of it all, the harshest of famines closed in on them.

In light of those conditions that appeared to spell the end of Beta Israel people, the people in Israel increasingly feared for the safety and life of the Beta Israel still remaining in that dangerous and lethal place. The Mossad was charged with finding a route out of Ethiopia and Sudan and a place for those Jews to gather and from which to flee safely to their traditional home, Jerusalem. Djibouti seemed to be the lesser of evils.

It had been a French territory, and the assessment by Mossad was that in as region like that—previously under liberal, democratic, European rule—the chances of success would be greater. There came to be a few Frenchmen who were in on the secret. In fact, towards the end, relying on the Frenchmen turned out to be a wise move.

Complications in the Djibouti plan and its execution soon arose, beginning in earnest when the police raided the villa safe house. For their own reasons, the Djibouti authorities came to believe that the villa's occupants were there to plan a coup. Nothing was spared to wring confessions out of the arrested group members, including prolonged torture. Later, when he was safe in Israel, Biro said,

"I was interrogated around the clock, bound and beaten. Questions kept coming nonstop. 'We came here to find work', was his stock answer, over and over."

After prolonged interrogation, threats, and beatings, the Beta Israel group was taken by their captors back to Ethiopia to Harari Prison where the questions and abuse became even harsher.

"If I could have taken my soul and thrown it into the garbage can, I would have done it. I could no longer take what I went through there. We all went through different forms of violence, including sexual abuse of both men and women, and whipping. At one point, I was struck in the eye by a whip and my vision has been blurred since. My right leg was also injured, and I have a permanent limp."

The group was in prison in Harari for four months, never having been charged, and not knowing when or even if, they would be released; and they had no information. They did not hear from the Mossad or the State of Israel. Then—one day—they were once again moved, this time to a prison in Addis Ababa known to insiders as "the end of the world". Every one of them feared that their lives would end there.

In that prison, for six months, they were subjected to continuing serious violence and mental anguish. Mamo Biro said of that time:

"There were ropes hanging in the center of the prison for executions. We slept below them, and occasionally people were hanged. To this day, when I see a dangling rope, I remember that… One day I and the rest of the group were told that we were being released. The person who got us out was the same Mossad man who had been our handler in Djibouti."

That man told Mamo that they were going to start the journey to Israel again. They were going to collect a new group and try to escape again, this time going through Sudan. However, by that time the route through Sudan had been shut down after being exposed in the news media. At least formally, that is. In actual practice, the Mossad still had a well-greased network that helped to get Ethiopian Jews to Israel during Operation Moses was still operating albeit limited in scope.

Mamo's group was taken in a shipping container to the middle of the desert, where a Hercules transport plane awaited them. With that, all members of his group made through Sudan and on to Israel, with one exception. Yeshiwork Dawit apparently did not make it out of the prison. Mamo presumed she had been murdered.

As it turned out, he was wrong about that. On the day the Djibouti troops stormed the house, Dawit was not there. The 13-year-old girl had been hospitalized a few days earlier with a serious case of pneumonia, and now she was wondering why no one was taking an interest in her.

"When a few days went by and no one from the group came to visit me, I got frightened," Yeshiwork recalled later.

Despite her condition, she left the hospital and went to the villa. As she approached the house, she heard someone shouting to her. It was the woman who had rented the house to them.

"They left; they all left," the woman told her.

The teenage girl did not get far; she was soon arrested by the police and imprisoned without charges, for what ended up to be more than a year.

"My children, my mother, no one has ever heard what I went through there in the jail. All the help I've received until now hasn't succeeded in letting me forget what they did to me there."

Yeshiwork was the youngest child in the facility, overseen by all male warders. She remembered weeping. They turned her into a sex slave. Everyone could do with her whatever they wanted, and they did things all the time, she related. They beat and raped her almost constantly. She spent 15 months there, and in all that time, no one told her why she had been imprisoned, where the other members of her group were, or when she might be freed, if ever. Like the others, incarceration ended without any prior notification.

"One day the doors opened; and they released a group of women; and I was one of them," she said.

Out of necessity, she then began a life on the streets of Djibouti City, sleeping in the open on cartons. She was also occasionally sexually assaulted.

"At any given moment, I didn't know where the next rape would come from."

At one point, she found a job as a housemaid. There, too, she as abused and raped, until she escaped back to the street. This time, she decided to return to the hospital in Djibouti where she had been treated for pneumonia; there she found a job as a cleaner and had a bed to sleep in for the first time in many months.

"I also found someone there who said he was going to Addis Ababa. I sent a letter with him to be forwarded to my mother; so, she would know I was alive."

The letter came as a complete surprise to her family. They had been told that she had died. In a few days after receiving the letter, a phone call reached the hospital. Yeshiwork was working at the time; it was the summer of 1987. She was summoned to answer the call for her, and the man on the line spoke Amharic. He was calling from Paris. She learned that he had been in touch with her family. The man told her that everyone knew she was alive, and that they were working to get her out of there. He told her she must do exactly as he told her. He instructed her to go to a certain place in town and get a passport photo taken and go quickly to the Ethiopian embassy to obtain a passport.

She obtained a passport and was told to go to the French embassy where a visa was already waiting for her. They sent her to the Air France office where she received a ticket to Paris. The entire process took only a few weeks.

She boarded the plane without difficulty and landed in Paris where she was met by the man on the phone, and a woman who told her they were representatives of Israel. That night, they put her on a plane for Israel. Her uncle was standing in the waiting area. She was debriefed and talked about everything to the agents, but she could not bring herself to say anything about the assaults.

The State of Israel did not acknowledge the Djibouti Operation. It was not until the 1990s that the group was finally recognized as "Prisoners of Zion."

"The state recognized that I was imprisoned and that I was a central activist working to encourage aliyah, but they don't want to recognize the trauma I've been carrying as a result. We were gathered together and sent into the fire... We were an experiment in a primitive cruel country. They made a mistake with us; and we were harmed; and no one is helping us to cope with that."

–Mamo Biro

"The path they took me on is something they didn't think about; they placed a girl in too much danger. They concentrated a group of more than 20 people in one house and thought we would not be exposed. They made mistakes, and we paid the price."

–Yeshiwork Dawi

Today, Biro is a father of three and lives in Nes Tziona. He is the custodian of a community center. Dawi eventually married and is the mother of three. She lives in Kiryat Malakhi and works as an assistant in a preschool.

In November, 2015—when it was estimated that 4,000 Beta Israel people remained trapped in Ethiopia and Sudan—the Israeli cabinet voted unanimously to allow the remaining Jews to be brought home to Israel. On March 11, 2021, 300 Ethiopian Jews made it to Israel–the last of 2,000 Jews known to remain in Ethiopia—having been transported during Operation Tzur Israel since 2020. As of June 14, 2022, 500 additional Black Jewish people made aliyah to Israel under Operation Dove Wing over the years 2010, 2015-2022.

As of the time of the writing of this book, more than 135,000 Beta Israel Ethiopian Jews live in Israel. The difficulties for the people and for the generous nation that took them in did not vanish by some magic upon their arrival in the safe haven. By the Law of Return, all of the immigrants were officially recognized as official Jews by most Rabbis and the government, which was their first hurdle upon entry to the small middle-eastern country.

Beta Israel people see themselves as no different whatsoever—other than the color of their skin—from the Yemenite, Iraqi, Moroccan, or Russian, communities already welcomed into Israel's society. They had survived pitched battles, battled poverty of the most extreme, endured forced conversions, and suffered cruel discrimination, while still holding to their identity as Jews. By the grace of God, and the Mossad, all but 10,000 of them have returned.

But people are people, and discrimination is, unfortunately, a very common attribute of people everywhere, including Israel. Beta Israel is different in multiple ways, and they are treated that way by many of their fellow Israelis. Assimilation of Ethiopian Jews into Israeli society has been a matter majority v. minority which is the equal to European and American association those two major factions.

A report by the Bank of Israel in 2006–and not much changed up to the present day– reveals serious discrepancies; only the high points will be covered here:

- The incidence of poverty among Ethiopians is ~51.7% compared with 15.8% in the general Israeli population.
- The rate of participation in the labor market is about 65.7% among adults compared with about 82.5% in the general population.
- Ethiopian unemployment is 13.2% compared with 7.4%.
- The monthly income per capita is estimated at about 1,994 NIS [New Israeli Shekels] v. 3,947.
- Students awarded the Bagrut certification is estimated at about 44% compared to 57%.
- Only about 34% meet the requirements needed for higher education, compared with about 83%.
- 21.7% of Ethiopian immigrants are holders of high school and higher education compared to 49.2%.
- About 20.4% of the immigrants are not holders of even a basic education as compared with 0.9% among the general population.
- In a 3002-2003 study, criminal charges brought against 20-30 twelve to twenty-year-old immigrants and only 4.6% in the general population, twice the number for the Ethiopians.

The Bank of Israel report also identified shortcomings in the government's efforts to integrate Ethiopians into the general society. Despite having spent 400,000 NIS per immigrant, plus private donations, local authority welfare systems, and by multiple contributors towards Affirmative Action schemes to help immigrants enter army or national service and other efforts to them to be included in higher education avenues; the success rate is regarded as being fair at best, and a dismal failure at worst.

The report recommended the following: that measures be taken to encourage immigrants to disperse around the country, rather than to remain concentrated in small homogeneous communities; that greater emphasis be placed on providing professional training to the immigrants; and that affirmative action be considered to aid their inclusion in public service jobs where presently discrimination hampers progress.

# Hero Jacob "Jake" B. Oldham 1996

Jacob "Jake" B. Oldham, 1996:

Very few Americans would recognize the name of Jake B. Oldham; but perhaps, we should. Jake came from Kaysville, Utah and was accepted in the Air Force Academy to gain his university education. The present author would have given his left arm to have the earned opportunity that Jake enjoyed. Beyond meeting all the requirements for admission, the young man was recognized as a modest, polite, person who always showed profound respect for others. He always stood up when his superiors walked into a room. He shook your hand and looked you in the eye.

In his first academy year—as an 18-year-old fourth-class cadet acting as a follower and functioning as cadet Airmen, a "doolie" (slave or servant)– he did well.But at the end of the first year, when he turned 19, he faced a personal crisis of the first order. Jake was an active member of the Church of Jesus Christ of Latter-day Saints [colloquially known as "Mormons"], and he and his family had always expected him to fulfill a religious proselytizing mission for the church when he came of age. The quandary for Jake was that the academy was not in the religion business; he had a commitment to the country, the air force, and to the academy. He was informed that if he left the air force university for two years, it was highly likely that he would not be able to return.

In practicality, Jake would have to reapply to the USAFA on the same footing as any other applicant, a truly daunting prospect, and a true test of his religious beliefs as well as his sense of honor and obligation to his country. He received a formal call to serve in Japan for two years including a period of learning the language and culture in the church's language training center.

Jake said he prayed about it... a lot. He concluded that it was something he had to do. For him, the decision was harsh; in order to leave for his church mission, he would have to resign from the academy and put in jeopardy his life-long academic and career dreams. He was told that it was likely that he would not be reaccepted, and his place would be taken by another.

Jake was a man of integrity, young as he was.

He said of his choice, "Some things are important enough that no matter how difficult, they are worth doing... My mission not only gave me an opportunity to love the Japanese people, and to share the gospel with them, but also it did a lot to help me to understand myself and to strengthen my testimony."

When he finished his mission, he had to face the stark reality that he might not be accepted back into the Academy. He was required to apply again just like any other aspiring student and to compete for a place with several thousand other applicants. His problem was compounded because he had to carry on his communications with the admissions committee in Colorado from Japan. His reputation for honor and integrity carried him through the process, and he re-accepted and returned to the Air Force Academy.

Jake Oldham graduated in May, 1996–and in so doing–achieved a place which makes him known to every person who attends the Academy. He was the Top Graduate, number one in his class for combined academic and military scores during his four years at the Academy. He graduated with a double major in pre-medicine and mechanical engineering and earned a place in the esteemed drum and bugle corps. He was one of four senior group commanders, a leader over 1000 other cadets. He sat in the first chair of 916 and was given a standing ovation by the professors, his military commanders, the appreciative audience, and most significantly, by his peers, the entire student body of the Air Force Academy. He was given the rare honor of having his name placed on the 100-year honor roll.

He stood up for and took serious personal risks for his religious beliefs and responsibilities. He proved himself to be a man of honor, a hero, in the definition used by this author. Dr. Jake Oldham later graduated from the Mayo Clinic in Rochester, Minnesota as a physician. He was, and is–a man of honor, a man true to himself.

## The Parents and Grandparents of Nickle Mines, Pennsylvania, Monday, April 2, 2006:

Someone told the present author that good writing should ignite anger, cause tears, or arouse emotions toward making things better. I felt all those emotions as I did the research for this remarkable set of true stories. I–like many Americans–have become no longer capable of keeping up with the sheer numbers of murderous outrages that seem to have increased in frequency to an average of one a week, let alone to remember the details of such heinous actions; so, we do not become inured or blasé and forget them.

The United States has had more mass shootings than any other country. *The Washington Post* recorded 163 mass shootings in the United States between 1967 and June, 2019. More than 352,000 students in 380 school shootings have experienced gun violence at school since Columbine High School on April 20, 1999. There have been 167 such shootings since 2018. 100s of thousands of families have been directly impacted. There were 35 school shootings in 2021, 10 in 2020, and 24 each in 2019 and 2018. There were 51 school shootings with injuries or deaths in 2022. Thus far [as of May 23, 2023], there have been 23 school shootings this year that resulted in injuries or deaths–34 people killed or injured in a school shooting; 12 people killed, including 8 students or other children killed; 4 school employees or other adults killed, and 22 people injured. Yet, according to recent US government statistics only about 2 percent of elementary schools in the US use metal detectors–7 percent of middle schools, and 10 percent of high schools.

Consider just two examples: On May 24, 2022, a mass shooting occurred at Robb Elementary School in Uvalde, Texas, United States. After shooting and severely wounding his mother at home, the killer fatally shot 19 students and two teachers. 17 others were injured but survived. For 45 minutes, the police ran the other way.

That should be enough to make you grit your teeth, hurl invectives, or shed tears. But, that is not the intention of the author. Rather, it is to compare, contrast, and to publicize a sliver of silver lining about living with such inexplicable violence in schools and otherwise. The keyword is forgiveness.

## Monday, October 2, 2006:

32-year-old Charles Carl Roberts IV—who lived in nearby Georgetown, another unincorporated area of Bart Township near the hamlet of Nickle Mines, Lancaster County, Pennsylvania—was an Englishman among Amish neighbors. He was a husband of Marie and father of two children, and he worked as a deliveryman for a milk company. Charlie was well known in the area. It was somewhat unusual for an English to make reciprocal friendships with the somewhat standoffish Amish, but Charlie was one of them. He and his family lived a quiet middle-class life. He had no criminal record or rap sheet. The only dark cloud in his life was the premature death of his daughter nine years previously. He never quite got over it.

On Monday morning, October 2, 2006–a beautiful clear day in Nickel Mines, Pennsylvania, a non-Amish man backed his pickup truck into the school yard of the West Nickel Mines Amish school. It was approximately 10:25 a.m. EDT, shortly after the children returned from recess. Inside the one-room schoolhouse were 28 students, and three adult women—the teacher and three visitors that day.

Survivors had told how–as Roberts brandished a Springfield Armory XD 9mm handgun–he ordered all the children to lie down at the front of the class, below the blackboard. Not just the girls. He ordered the boys to help him carry items into the classroom from the truck. In the early confusion, young Zook and her mother–who was visiting–took the opportunity to escape and ran toward a nearby farm for help. Roberts saw them leave, and ordered one of the boys to stop them, threatening to shoot everyone if they got away. They reached the farm, where they asked Amos Smoker to call 9-1-1. At 10:35 a.m., Amos Smoker called 911 for the schoolteacher, Emma Mae Zook. About the time of this initial call for help, the shooter released a pregnant woman, three parents with infants, and all 15 male students.

Meanwhile, at the school, the boys carried in lumber, a shotgun, a stun-gun, wires, chains, nails, tools, a small bag, and wooden board with multiple sets of metal eye-hooks. The bag held a change of clothes, toilet paper, candles, and flexible plastic ties. Using wooden boards, Roberts barricaded the front door. He had prepared for a lengthy siege.

Apparently startled that his plans appeared to be going awry, Roberts ordered the remaining adults and boys out of the school. He nailed the door shut and pulled the blinds to darken the room. He tied together the legs of the remaining ten girls, who were still lying on the floor at the front of the room. When Roberts began tying the girls up and pulled down the window shades, Aaron Esh Sr. said, children began weeping with fear.

"The boys were terrified, too," he said, rubbing his ample beard.

Just before he barricaded himself and the girls inside, Roberts let the boys go. One girl, nine-year-old Emma Fisher, escaped without her older sister. Aaron Jr. went outside, then panicked because his little brother Joel was still inside. Joel–then seven–was the last boy out. Seven minutes after the teacher raised the alarm, state troopers arrived.

By 11:00 a.m. a large crowd–including police officers, emergency medical technicians, and residents of the village–had assembled both outside the schoolhouse and at a nearby ambulance staging area.

It is believed Roberts planned to molest the girls sexually during a lengthy siege. K-Y Jelly–a lubricant most commonly used for sexual intercourse–was also found in the schoolhouse among Roberts' belongings, possibly suggesting multiple motives for the incident. He told them–survivors said–that he was angry at God and could not forgive himself because his baby daughter had died despite his prayers. He also said he had molested two young female relatives while a teenager, a claim that was never proved, and that he could not forgive God; and he could not forgive himself.

By this time, police had begun arriving at the school, responding to a phone call the distraught teacher had made after running a half mile to the neighboring farmhouse. Realizing the police had arrived and were asking him–through a bullhorn, to surrender–Roberts himself called 911, telling the responder that he would shoot everyone if the police did not leave.

A 13-year-old Amish girl named Marian Fisher asked to be shot first in an attempt to buy time for the younger students, according to a close family friend.

The girl's 11-year-old sister, Barbara, affectionately known as "Barbie", then said, "Shoot me next."

Anna Mae Stoltzfus, age 12, was reported to have added, "Then, shoot me."

The younger Fisher girl, Barbie, survived five bullet wounds in the assault and told her family what happened from her bed at Children's Hospital of Philadelphia, where she was being treated for wounds to her shoulder, hand and leg.

Marian had been bound with the other children by Charles Carl Roberts IV in the West Nickel Mines Amish School.

"They were already tied up; they knew they were going to be shot."

Marian and Barbie's pleas allowed the girls a little extra time for possible rescue. But, after firing a shot through a window at the police, he fired at each of the 10 girls, then shot himself dead. But, at approximately 11:07 a.m., Roberts implemented his threats, and the sound of rapid gunfire was heard. He got off 13 shots in 8 seconds. Then, it was silent.

The rampage killed five of the defenseless little girls and severely injured the other five. Three of the girls were shot execution-style in the back of the head, with one dying in the arms of a trooper. The deputy coroner in Lancaster County, Pennsylvania, counted at least a dozen shotgun pellet inflicted wounds in one child alone before asking a colleague to take over and continue for her. There was not one desk, not one chair, in the whole schoolroom that was not splattered with either blood or glass. There were bullet holes everywhere.

The Amish still eschew cars and do not rely on phones, factors which meant that at the time, news of the shooting was slow to reach parents. Roberts had three children and a wife, for whom he left four separate suicide notes.

The community convulsed in shock and grief. The boys had a lucky escape; so, everyone said. But they were also severely traumatized. Roberts ordered all the boys to leave and then shot the girls.

The shooter's wife Marie Roberts released a statement on the night of the shootings to the media saying: "The man who did this today is not the Charlie that I've been married to for almost 10 years. My husband is loving, supportive, thoughtful, all the things you'd always want and more. Our hearts are broken, our lives are shattered, and we grieve for the innocence and lives that were lost today."

Mrs. Roberts—the killer's mother–described the horror of her experience: "By that time I was at my son's home, and I saw my husband and the state trooper standing right in front of me as I pulled in. And I looked at my husband, he said, 'It was Charlie', he said, 'I will never face my Amish neighbors again.'"

But she is invited to gatherings and often visits Rosanna King, who was six when Charles Roberts shot her. She is confined to a wheelchair, unable to talk and fed through a tube. She has seizures.

Yet–when members of the Amish community traveled to see and to bring solace and food to the Roberts family–one Amish man held Roberts' sobbing father in his arms for an hour to comfort him.

Later, Marie Roberts wrote an open letter to her Amish neighbors thanking them for their forgiveness, grace, and mercy. She wrote, "Your love for our family has helped to provide the healing we so desperately need. Gifts you've given have touched our hearts in a way no words can describe. Your compassion has reached beyond our family, beyond our community, and is changing our world, and for this we sincerely thank you."

Esh's father, Aaron Esh Sr, said, "Aaron had survivor's guilt; he lost his childhood that day. It bothered him and other boys that they had not done something. Some of them were still struggling with that, 10 years on. In the months afterwards, he said, his son "always had a fear that it would happen again".

Within days, the community knocked down the schoolhouse. In April, 2007, Esh Sr. said, when they had just finished building a new school and moved the surviving children there, "Virginia Tech happened". In Blacksburg, Virginia, a disturbed student killed 32 students and members of staff. Many in Nickel Mines were distressed all over again.

At 23, Aaron Esh Jr still carried the weight of the terrible events of a day 10 years before. He was the oldest student present. Aaron Esh Jr. sat in his gas-lit family kitchen to talk to reporters. From outside came the sound of rain and horse-drawn carriages on a country road. In all directions, the rolling landscape was dotted with grain silos, cornfields, and barns.

For a long time, Esh had wrestled with himself, tormented by the idea that he could somehow have saved his classmates. He still struggles with the memories. Survivor's guilt.

"That hit Aaron real hard," Esh Sr. said.

Aaron Jr's mother, Anna Mary, said her son became very good at cooking for the rest of the family, but ate nothing himself.

"We couldn't get him to eat," she said.

Aaron Jr went through a growth spurt that winter, growing from 5" 1' to 5" 6', but his weight dropped from 120 pounds to 90 pounds.

"He was completely anorexic. He was like a toothpick," Esh Sr. said.

The boy would come home early from school, having panic attacks. Like most of the survivors and bereaved, he and his brother accepted counselling from outside professional therapists. But Aaron Jr was depressed. In the summer of 2007, he ended up in a secure hospital ward, close to death from starvation. He spent many painful months recovering, the family said.

"The only way it was explained to us was that he couldn't control what had happened in his life that day, but there was something he could control and that was what he ate," Esh Sr said.

Aaron Jr said that around that time, three state troopers came to visit him. They sat outside on the porch, he said, and told him what happened at the school was not his fault. If he had tried to intervene, they said, the outcome would probably have been a lot worse.

"It meant so much to me to hear it from them," he said. "It saved my sanity. If it hadn't been for that I don't know how I would have handled it. At one point I had had thoughts of suicide."

Talking on the next Thursday on their sprawling dairy farm–where they raise 40 cows on pasture, corn and alfalfa and also grow tobacco– the girls' parents, John and Linda Fisher, said no one had been able to figure out exactly what their daughter Marian meant. At the time, Marian was widely held to have displayed superhuman courage, in an attempt to protect the younger girls. Now, the truth remains something of a mystery. John Fisher said Barbie had said her sister's face was full of distress, not stoicism, when she spoke.

The attacker preyed on the most innocent and defenseless members of a determinedly bucolic and pacifistic religious community. The ages of the victims ranged from six to thirteen. Within hours, the Amish announced they had forgiven Roberts.

None of those affected by "the happening"–as the community calls it–have left the tight-knit community or the Amish faith itself, Stoltzfus said. Their old-world way of life has not changed.

Within 30 minutes this event literally became news around the world. Not–it should be noted–because male violence against girls was newsworthy—that theme, in fact, was seemingly lost in the reporting that followed or was assumed unfortunately to be commonplace. Instead, the story that first flew around the globe was that the last safe place the rest of the world had imagined—rural Amish schools—had just been added to the growing list of school shootings sites.

But very quickly the media story shifted from one of lost innocence to one of bewilderment and even consternation. The victimized Amish community, it seemed to many observers, was reacting in strange ways.

They also said the decision by the community to forgive the killer and his family was not as simple as it has been seen to be.

"It's not a once and done thing," said Linda Fisher. "It is a lifelong process."

As a principle, forgiveness is closely adhered to by the Amish. But it takes a while for each person's emotions to catch up with such an outward decision, John Fisher said. When he saw the wounded girls fighting for their lives in the hospital, he was angry.

"That's when it hit me," he said. "As a father, I felt helpless."

Two sisters survived until the early hours of October 3 when their life support was ended.

Within a few hours of the shooting members of the local Amish community reached out in sympathy to his widow, his parents, his parents-in-law, assuring them that they would not scapegoat them for what happened. Six days later–when most non-Amish neighbors stayed away from Roberts' burial–the Amish did not, and ended up being half of the mourners present, and again hugged his family and cried together. They included Amish parents who had just the day before buried their own daughters in customary Amish tradition; guests brought food, not flowers. A hymn was read in 16th century German, but there was no singing.

The dead were laid in simple pine coffins and dressed in homemade white dresses, symbolizing purity. Two sermons were given, both in

Pennsylvania Dutch. After the 90-minute service, about 300 men with long beards and women in white bonnets climbed into their black and gray buggies and clip-clopped in quiet procession to Bart Amish Cemetery. Along the way, they passed the house of Charles C. Roberts IV, the 32-year-old killer.

During the initial investigation, a stone-faced deputy county coroner, Amanda Shelley, described for reporters the blood on the walls of the one-room schoolhouse where the rampage occurred. But her composure dissolved when she mentioned a sign hanging beneath the chalkboard. It read, "Visitors Brighten People's Days."

About the same time, the ad hoc Amish committee set up to oversee the money that poured in from around the world for the shooting victims announced that they would be diverting some of the money to a second fund for the Roberts family. Now that was news. And it was a story that reporters—and the public at large—was unprepared for. They did not know what to make of it. Forgiveness of this sort was so uncommon.

Some people praised Amish forgiveness and jumped to apply its example to a host of other social and political issues. Others denounced Amish forgiveness, condemning it as too fast, emotionally unhealthy, and a denial of innate human need to seek revenge. People of the Amish culture believe forgiveness is a good thing, but a difficult and complex thing.

As it turns out, the Amish have a far from simplistic understanding of forgiveness. True, some things were clear from the start: The decision to forgive came quickly, instinctively. The Amish knew they wanted to forgive, knew it so clearly that they could express it immediately and publicly even if and while they did not feel that way. One Amish grandmother laughed when asked if there had been a meeting to decide if the gunman should be forgiven. No, she and others said, forgiveness was a decided matter—decided long before October 2 ever raised the occasion for forgiveness.

At the same time, this grandmother and others made clear that forgiving is hard work, emotionally, and that deciding to forgive and expressing that desire with words and actions are only a first step. Many of those close to the tragedy made use of professional counselors and, years later, continue to work with their grief. The Amish drew on the resources of both professionals and of their culture and faith. As they explain forgiveness, they usually use biblical language to explain that forgiveness is a long process: Jesus said that even small offenses need to be forgiven seventy times seven, they note, suggesting that forgiving takes time and is not a simple once-and-done event.

"You think about them, you cry about them, you pray for them," said Lizzy Fisher, an Amish grandmother who is close to several great-grandparents of the slain girls. "And then you have to let go of things you can't explain."

It's important here to clarify what the Amish believe forgiveness is and is not: it is not pretending that nothing happened or that the offense was not so bad in the cosmic order of things. More importantly, it is not pardon. i.e., it is not to say there should be no consequences for actions. Had Charles Roberts lived, the Amish no doubt would have supported his prosecution and imprisonment for the sake of everyone's safety.

Instead—in the culture—forgiveness is about giving up: giving up your right to revenge. And giving up feelings of resentment, bitterness, and hatred, replacing them with compassion toward the offender.And treating the offender as a fellow human being. It is a direct compliance with the command of Jesus.

It is hard work, even if the decision to forgive is settled. When a grieving grandfather, asked by reporters less than 48 hours after two of his granddaughters had been slain if he had forgiven the killer, responded, "In my heart, yes," his words conveyed a commitment to move toward forgiveness, offered with the faith that loving feelings would eventually replace distraught and angry ones.

Speaking the folk wisdom of experience, Amish people told reporters, "The acid of hate destroys the container that holds it."And, "It's not good to hold grudges. Why not let go, give it up and not let the person [who wronged you] have power over you."

Forgiving may be about self-denial, but it is not self-loathing. In fact, forgiving, the Amish affirm, is good for you, not just for the person forgiven. The Amish explanation of forgiveness is more complicated than many of the popular presentations of Amish forgiveness that suggested they stoically stuffed their feelings in a box.

The first rule Amish cite for their concentration on forgiveness is theological: Jesus tells each of us to forgive, and God expects to comply. The Amish immediately point to Jesus parables on forgiveness and especially to the Lord's Prayer, with its key line:Forgive us as we forgive others.

It is not uncommon in the Lancaster, Pennsylvania settlement for Amish people to recite the Lord's Prayer eight times a day, and ten times on Sundays.The Amish there strongly discourage composing original prayers and use only the original written prayers routinely and liturgically. As well, they point out that the line forgive us as we forgive others is the only part of the Lord's Prayer that Jesus underscores. Immediately following the Prayer, Jesus says: "For if you forgive others their trespasses your heavenly Father will also forgive you; but if you do not forgive others, neither will your heavenly Father forgive your trespasses." And we all trespass.

The Amish believe that God's forgiveness of them is dependent on their forgiving others. Forgiveness becomes a religious obligation for the Amish people. The principle is rooted in sound scientific principles. The were 950 studies on the subject by 2005. 20+ years ago, the concept of forgiveness was considered to be the domain of religion, a topic for the pulpit but not for academic study or even psychotherapy. Then researchers showed that the inability to forgive has an impact on health–on blood pressure, immune response, and depression, for example; and scientists started paying attention.

There are two kinds of forgiveness, they say: decisional and emotional. A person may choose to forgive another person; but if he is still feeling bitter, it has not been an emotional forgiveness and is incomplete. Follow-up studies of the Amish parents who immediately forgave the man who shot 10 schoolgirls in October, 2006, show that they still express difficulty dealing with the losses emotionally.

Anger, anxiety, fear, and a narcissistic sense of entitlement, also contribute to a person's inability to forgive, as does a person's tendency to ruminate. The misperception that the Amish had quickly gotten over the tragedy was one of many about the community, according to Jonas Beiler, the founder of the Family Resource and Counseling Center.

Author's note: My wife asked a pertinent question about what she perceived to be an inconsistency in the Amish culture which makes understanding of the great act of forgiveness all that more confusing. Their reaction to the hellish Nickel Mines School shooting gives every evidence that the Amish are a gracious, forgiving people. But, they also hold to a principle of forgiving/punishment called shunning. Some commentators picked up on this inconsistency with the obvious question. How can the Amish, so forgiving in one context, be so judgmental in another?

One of the most controversial aspects of the Amish is their practice of shunning or applying "the ban." Shunning means breaking most forms of social contact with excommunicated members or those who leave the Amish after becoming members. Amish are not permitted to eat at the same table as a shunned member nor to accept any gifts, rides, or other services, from them. The exact boundaries of interaction are different from one Amish community to the next, but shunning always involves a strict and intentionally painful degree of separation from the community, including family members. The purpose of shunning is to protect the community by separating out any negative influence while also ideally using the shame and pain of separation to draw the person back into proper fellowship. If the shunned member returns to their community in contrition, they will–after a time–be received back into the community.

Shunning is a practice of social exclusion and discipline that applies to church members only who break community rules or leave the church and/or community. It is based on biblical passages—see *Matthew 18:15-18* and *1st Corinthians 5:13*–and aims to maintain the integrity of the Amish church and encourage the repentance of offenders.

Shunning applies only to baptized members, and the Amish only baptize adults into the church. Amish parents never have to shun their young children because young children cannot be registered members of an Amish church. The Amish also do not shun outsiders or even family members that never choose to receive baptism, though their relationships with adults who are not members of the Amish church are always somewhat limited. Amish are admonished at least three times and given chances to repent before they are shunned. Amish members can be shunned for three broad reasons:

- **Unrepentant Sin**: In a sense, the Amish would say that this is the only reason they shun a person.
- **Unrepentant Violation of the Community Rules**: Every Amish community has what is called an "Ordnung"—a community rule that governs what technologies are restricted, what a person may wear, trades a person may work, what forms of recreation are allowed, and a host of other details of daily life. The Ordnung is not, in theory, viewed as being an infallible moral law such as adultery, murder, or stealing. Cars, electricity, colored clothing, or even buttons, or belts, are not–in and of themselves, though frowned upon–necessarily sins. They are nonetheless important because they are things each Amish community has decided on as guardrails of separation from the world. However, as a matter of principle, the Amish see it as sinful for an Amish member to violate their own community's Ordnung; it is a sin of pride and divisiveness. Violating the Ordnung is considered sin because it violates the Amish baptismal vow. Every Amish member has to take a vow as part of their baptism. That vow includes a promise to keep the community Ordnung, and you are sinning by breaking your vow.
- **Leaving the Amish**: This command is applied somewhat differently from one Amish community to the next. Many Amish will remove the ban and discontinue shunning the person if they join and remain faithful to a like-minded church, such as a different Amish sect or a conservative Mennonite church. Stricter Amish sects, however, insist that one must remain faithful to the church in which one was baptized and therefore will shun even a person who moves to and joins a neighboring Amish community. Again, this is argued primarily based on the assumption of prideful motives and on the Amish baptismal vow. One might find themselves shunned for having attended the service of a non-Amish Christian church or a local evangelical revival meeting because this violated the Ordnung.

The answer lies in the distinction between forgiveness and pardon, as described above.

*Forgiveness* refers to a victim's commitment to forgo revenge and to replace anger (toward the offender) with love and compassion. *Pardon*–on the other hand–refers to the dismissal of disciplinary consequences that ensue from the offense. This distinction between forgiveness and pardon is not unique to the Amish; in fact, it appears as a matter of course in the psychological literature on forgiveness—a literature that is pioneered by Robert Enright at the University of Wisconsin-Madison. Forgiveness is an act of mercy toward an offender, writes Enright, but granting forgiveness (as defined above) does not necessarily mean that justice will be bypassed. Pardoning an offense may—or may not—accompany the act of forgiveness.

Other faiths have rules or laws regarding forgiveness and pardoning. With regards Islam, see the articles on Ebrahim Mohebi, and Samareh Ali Nezhad [Alinejad] and AbdolqaniHossein Zadeh, elsewhere in this volume. Sharia law in Islam provides a select and specific form of forgiveness. The grieving parent of a murdered family member may overturn a sentence of execution for a murderer, but otherwise, the convicted perpetrator must still suffer the other judicial punishments ordered by the Sharia judge.

In general, Christian sects do not inflict judicial punishments for crimes under civil law against individuals or the state, nor do they exercise any right to pardon. Individuals may forgive, and sects may inflict religious punishments such as excommunication, a diluted form of shunning. As an example, The Church of Jesus Christ of Latter-day Saints regularly holds "church courts" to determine guilt or innocence of a church member for any serious violation of church or civil rules or laws. The maximum punishment is excommunication—and, even then—the excommunication may be lifted after repentance. The "guilty" member is not shunned by other members or family, but may lose church privileges, such as taking the "sacrament" [elsewhere known as the eucharist], temple attendance, or holding important church positions.

Forgiveness is certainly not exclusive to religions or religious believers, and not just to the Amish. Individuals may forgive other individuals as a matter of choice; and in some instances, that may carry over into the criminal justice system decisions.

## Chris Williams

A drunk teenage driver killed the wife and two children of an innocent family headed by **Chris Williams**. Two cars collided on a February night; the impact spun around the Volkswagen Passat driven by Williams and smashed it into a bridge support under the freeway. After the screeching and the thud, the shocking groan of metal hitting metal and then concrete, the only sound in the cold night was the insistent revving of the Passat's engine.

Chris once worked as a hospital orderly; so, he could immediately see his future. In the back seat were the deep, bloodless gashes in 11-year-old Ben's face, and the motionless body of 9-year-old Anna. As he watched, his pregnant wife Michelle gave her last, sad exhalation. Williams himself was in so much pain it was a struggle even to turn the key in the ignition. In the minutes before the ambulances arrived–as horrified passers-by tried to extricate him–Williams put his head back and moaned.

But then a strange thought rose to the surface: "Whoever has done this to us, I forgive them. I don't care what the circumstances were, I forgive them."

It was not just a random thought in the mind of dazed and grief-stricken man; it was a determinative decision.

Later, police found a dazed 17-year-old boy several blocks from the scene. Police estimate that Cameron White had been going at least 60 mph and was drunk on vodka when his car came down the hill on 2000 East, heading straight for the Williams' family car, killing Williams's wife, two of his children, and severely injuring a third. Still, Williams held fast to his decision to forgive.

Like all examples of extravagant forgiveness, that decision was both a simple resolution and an epic, complicated journey–one that could confound those among us who imagine how vengeful we might feel in the face of such a horrific loss.

## Gary Ceran

Another grieving father, Gary Ceran, publicly forgave a different drunken man who killed his wife and two of his children in a Taylorsville, Utah intersection on Christmas Eve, 2006. Chris Williams made headlines in February when he publicly forgave White.

In March, another grieving parent, Anna Kei'aho, stunned a courtroom full of onlookers when she forgave the man who had gunned down her son. In October, Ben Howard of Huntsville, Utah stood up in a Layton courtroom and requested leniency for the driver who slammed into his van on Highway 89, killing his wife and two of his children, a request that made the judge and court bailiff cry.

The fact that these acts of forgiveness surprise us is a reminder of how difficult an act it is. In a world where old grudges erupt daily in roadside bombs and recent reactions lead to road rage shootings, to forgive may or may not be divine, but it is not always human nature either.

The rest of the Williams story provides a glimpse into the reason for Chris's choice. Years earlier–when Chris Williams was 16–a little boy had run out onto 8th Avenue and into the path of his car. And so, the night half his family died–after White was apprehended–Williams remembered what it was like to be a teenager all alone in the back of a police car. But his desire to forgive had less to do with his own experience as a teenager who had killed a child, he says, and more to do with what by then had become a kind of practice.

"It was almost like I had drilled myself for that moment," he said.

Part of his training included a prayer he used to say after his first son, Michael, was born: "Help me appreciate him, and if he's taken prematurely, give me strength."

Three years ago, when Michael nearly died of toxic shock syndrome, Williams said the same prayer. The point, he says, is that none of us is entitled to a perfect life. Really understanding that is central to being able to forgive. To think that things will always work out in our favor is to set ourselves up for anger, at other people and at God.

There are now scores of people researching forgiveness, producing 950 studies as of 2005, up eightfold from eight years earlier. Before Dr. Robert Enright of the University of Wisconsin launched the field 20 years ago, though, the concept of forgiveness was considered the domain of religion, a topic for the pulpit but not for academic study or even psychotherapy. Then researchers showed that the inability to forgive has an impact on health: on blood pressure, immune response and depression, for example; and people started paying attention.

There are two kinds of forgiveness, according to the study: decisional and emotional. So, a person may choose to forgive another person; but if he is still feeling bitter, it has not been a full and cleansing emotional forgiveness. Follow-up studies of the Amish parents who immediately forgave the man who shot 10 schoolgirls in October, 2006 show that "they still express difficulty dealing with the losses emotionally," their therapists said

Another example is worthy of more detail–the parents of Ann Grosmaire—Kate and Andy. On Sunday, March 28, 2010, the couple was gardening in their Tallahassee, Florida home's backyard. It was a nice day of working in the sun, and they were comfortably tired. Both were washing up when the doorbell rang. The Leon County deputy sheriff and another woman stood there, and they immediately knew something was wrong.

They told Kate and Andy that their 19-year-old daughter Ann had been shot. They could not even comprehend those words at first. It had to be something minor; that everything would be okay. Kate thought maybe the baby store she worked for had been robbed, but it was closed on Sundays. She was supposed to be with her boyfriend Conor.

"Was Conor with her?" Kate asked.

"Conor McBride?" the deputy sheriff said. "Conor is the one who shot her."

The impact could hardly have been worse. Ann was the youngest of their three girls, and Kate always knew she would be her last baby. She nursed her little girl until she was 18 months old.

As a teenager, Ann loved theater; she met Conor in drama class, was always directing and serving on tech crew. During her senior year, she performed a starring role in a play. Ann adored babies. Many days, she would text us photos of toys and foot jammies while working at the baby store. She had a special love for Sophie the Giraffe. Ann dreamed of one day finding a piece of land to raise horses and rescue birds of prey. She frequently spoke of her exciting life ahead.

She and Conor started dating as sophomores at Leon High School. After graduation, they both enrolled at Tallahassee Community College. The Grosmaires liked Conor. He was an honor student and in a leadership program. He was always very polite and well spoken. Andy and Kate believed would be their son-in-law someday.

The young couple argued a lot, but Kate remembered that she was a teenager once and could relate to Ann's powerful emotions. Ann's parents did not realize, however, how intense their arguments could be, or that they lacked the grown-up skills to know when to walk away.

After talking to the police, the Grosmaires raced to Tallahassee Memorial Hospital, where the doctor gave them the chilling truth: Ann had been shot at close range through her right eye with a shotgun. Their baby lay on a hospital bed with machines keeping her alive. She had some meager brainstem function but needed a ventilator to breathe.

Various doctors came by for consultations. Her skull had been left open by the neurosurgeon to deal with her brain swelling. A reconstructive specialist talked the Grosmaires through what could be done for her injured hand. A bandage covered the lost fingers of her hand, which she had instinctively raised to protect herself. After that was stabilized, the specialist would do what he could to salvage her hand. Kate doubted she would survive the week; dealing with her hand sadly seemed low on the list.

Andy asked the doctor if he could touch her, worried that he might make her precarious condition worse.

*"How could that be possible?"* Kate wondered to herself.

At 10 p.m. that night, the hospital was quiet. Andy came into the intensive-care room with a man who looked vaguely familiar. It was Michael McBride, Conor's father.

Kate sat across from Ann's bed and thought, *Can I go to him?"*

She stood up and walked across the room.

Then another question popped into her head, *"Can I embrace him?"*

She did. Ever afterwards, Kate says that it had to have been God's grace that walked her across that room because I don't know how I would have done it otherwise.

Once she hugged him, Michael said simply, "I'm so sorry."

Kate took advantage of the fact that her name was one of the five allowed to visit him. In jail, Conor could put four names on a list. Going down to see him that first time, she said her stomach was in knots. The room was stark and simple with glass panes and little plastic chairs and telephones.

Conor sat down on the other side of the glass, picked up the phone, and said, "I'm so, so, so, sorry."

He was crying.

"Conor, Mr. Grosmaire wants me to tell you that he loves you and forgives you," Ann's mother said. "You know I love you. And I forgive you."

Kate thought he was surprised to hear her say that.

Kate knew it was just a matter of time before Ann was gone. That reality took longer to sink in for her husband. Slowly, her organs were failing; and doctors told us things were not working the way they should. A stream of other visitors prayed with them and brought snacks. Later that night, Kate watched a nurse tend to her injuries and check her vital signs. Caring for Ann had always been Kate's job, but her injuries were far past what I could fix with Neosporin and a kiss. She ruminated that she would never again be able to reach out and have that hand grasp hers.

Andy Grosmaire is the Chief of Licensing with the Office of Financial Regulation for the state of Florida and a permanent deacon in the Catholic Church serving the diocese of Pensacola-Tallahassee. Kate Grosmaire is a Business Analyst with the Florida Department of Environmental Protection. Both are level-headed, religious believers.

Finally, Andy and Kate went to speak with their priest. They told him that the Ann they love and know was gone. They asked what were the Church's teachings on withdrawing life support? They did not want to prolong the inevitable or watch our daughter suffer further.

They decided to take Ann off life support on April 2. But before they actually did that, Kate knew she needed to see Conor. It is what her daughter would have wanted. No one ever fully recovers from the death of a child. But Kate wanted to be someone who was happy and not hiding from the world, bitter, and angry. Forgiveness was the way to peace; she and her priest knew she would need that.

Conor asked how Ann was doing, and she spoke carefully: "She's holding her own."

Kate knew that she would very soon be disconnected from her life support, but she could not tell him that. We could never talk about anything related to the case; so, there was little to talk about, she said.

Kate returned to the hospital. Ann's best friend Khadijah had come to spend some time with her. Ann's sisters–Sarah, 32, and Allyson, 28–also went in for a while. Then, it was time for them all to say a last "goodbye." Slowly, her organs were failing and doctors told the family things were not working the way they should.

When the doctors and nurses took Ann off life support, Kate and Andy had planned on moving her to hospice, expecting it to take awhile. But when the couple returned to the room, she was not breathing. She was very still. Kate held her hand, feeling her pulse slow. In the end, it was very quick–not hours or days. It was not even five minutes from the time they took the tube out until she was dead.

Andy came around the side of the bed and picked her up, held her to his chest, and wept. As Kate cried, a song came to her, and she sang, filling the quiet room. It felt right to send her off with her favorite gospel song, Angel Band. The Grosmaires came to realize that there was a small miracle—something of a silver lining–Ann was taken from a place of violence, where she was all alone, and brought to the hospital so that we could all come. Her aunts and uncles and cousins came. They were able to say "goodbye" and be by her side.

The next major issue in the drama was about the trial and sentencing of Conor. In Florida, there is a policy of 10-20-life, which means that if you just have a gun and commit a crime, you are sentenced to 10 years. If it discharges, you are sentenced to 20 years. And if you harm or kill someone, it is 25 years to life. There was a little bit of comfort in knowing that the state of Florida was going to take care of this. Conor would spend the rest of his life in prison, and Ann's parents did not even have to think about it.

But two months after Ann's death, they met with the assistant state attorney, Jack Campbell. He discussed the process and how he would handle it all. They would not have to testify. Campbell also explained that even mandatory minimums were negotiable. He could charge Conor with manslaughter and recommend five years. That sentence came as a bolt of lightening.

Seeing the couple's reaction, he quickly said, "Oh no, I would never do that. We're looking at 40 years or life."

That night, Kate could not sleep. It was one thing to say, "Poor Conor. He has to spend the rest of his life in jail."

But her nagging response to herself was, "But if he doesn't have to, what am I going to do about that?"

She was all about a meaningful sentence. Only 4% of inmates in the Florida correctional system have jobs while they are in prison. Through the night, Kate struggled with the idea of this young, smart, able-bodied, man sitting in a jail cell, not doing anything productive for the rest of his life. How could that be any kind of compensation to her and Andy for the loss of their daughter?

She focused on a more meaningful sentence–like having Conor serve half his time incarcerated and then the other half doing community service in the areas that Ann would have wanted. What Conor did was horrible, they reasoned, but did they want to be defined by their worst moment? Did they want that to be the way they lived the rest of their lives?

Together, they arrived at a greatest hope for Conor: to help get him into the faith and community-based prison Wakulla, just south of Tallahassee. They met with an Episcopal priest, Allison DeFoor, who worked in the prison system. He asked why they were not pursuing restorative justice. We had never heard that term before. Andy got *The Little Book of Restorative Justice*, and it captivated him. In a restorative justice conference, the victims have a voice. They can confront the offender and say what the offense meant to them, how it affected their lives. When they can explain that to the offender, the offender then gains empathy.

In the process, the offender also has to be willing to accept responsibility for what he or she did. That can be a tough sell. But when the offender can listen to a victim, accept responsibility, and also participate in sentencing, then they are more likely to complete the sentence as model prisoners and less likely to offend again. The process has the potential to change everybody in the room.

Andy and Conor's father, Michael, started meeting for lunch every week. They had both lost children in this horrible event. They discussed how restorative justice could be a way to help Conor. It was going to be a challenge to make a restorative justice conference happen in Florida. First, we had no legal authority even to suggest it. And second, it had never been done with a capital murder charge in the state. It was mostly used for juvenile offenses and minor felonies.

Andy wanted to know all about the events of that dreadful day, what the argument was about, to hear what Ann's last words were, and hopefully to gain some useful understanding. Kate wanted people to know who Ann was. This was a way for me to participate in the process and to have a say in how they felt Conor should be sentenced.

Finally, on June 22, 2011–a little more than 14 months since Ann's death–they came together for a restorative justice circle. Those were five of the most intense hours in all their lives. The little conference room in the prison held 12 plastic chairs. It was very plain: linoleum floor, concrete block walls, and long slit windows. Ann's best friend had knitted her an afghan; so, we put that in the center of the circle, along with other things that reminded them of Ann.

Conor came in and hugged his parents, then he hugged the Gosmaires. Jack Campbell read the charges against Conor. Father Mike said a prayer.

Then Andy and Kate spoke to everyone about Ann's life–from the time she was born, how Kate knew she would be her last baby. They told of small things: Ann had a lazy eye and wore a patch as a child. She loved her guinea pigs and her horse, and she wanted to have her own animal rehabilitation center after college. Andy talked earnestly about how she was just 19 and was going to be going to the University of Central Florida in the fall to finish her degree.

The hardest part for Kate was talking about the children Ann would never have. Ann worked at a baby boutique and loved children. It was very difficult for her to talk about that in such a place at such a time.

Conor listened. He listened to all of it.

After that, it was his turn.

He said, "Ann and I would fight sometimes, because I didn't understand the things that were important to her. She'd get disappointed in me."

Monday the 2nd was no different. They had fought on Friday night, but Ann had made the dean's list and planned a picnic for them on Saturday. When they went, Conor was not very enthusiastic. They argued most of that night, too, and through the following morning. Both teens were exhausted.

Finally, Ann said she was leaving. Conor did not know whether she meant for that day or for good; but she left her water bottle; and he followed to the car to give it to her.

When he asked what she wanted from him, she cried, "I wish you were dead!"

He went back inside, loaded his father's shotgun, and put the barrel under his chin. He wondered, *If I kill myself, would Ann blame herself?* Just then, Ann knocked on the door, begging to be let in and interrupting him. When she found out what he was trying to do, she told him she did not want to live either.

This was the moment when they could have changed the story. But neither of them had the maturity to walk away. Conor told police and the Gosmaires how he picked the gun back up, wanting to threaten her with it. She was sitting on her knees on the bedroom floor. He waved it around, tired of arguing and tired of everything. He asked Ann if that was what she wanted. She said no, but he said he pointed the gun at her and pulled the trigger. He immediately regretted what happened, but it was too late.

Right then, Jack Campbell called for a break and asked if the parents wanted to quit. But the Gosmaires had just heard the worst part. Andy had come to make sense of what happened. Kate wanted to continue because she wanted to have a say in his sentencing.

They all went back in. Conor continued his narrative by saying he considered killing himself right then but could not bring himself to do it.

When he walked into the Tallahassee Police Department that day, he told police, "I just killed my fiancé, and you need to give me the death penalty."

That was his mindset. He had killed her; so, his life was forfeit.

A restorative justice circle typically ends with a discussion about punishment. Kate told Sujatha Baliga–the restorative justice lawyer–she would recommend a term of five years. After listening to the details, Kate was not sure she could still ask for a five-year sentence.

But she was determined, and she said it right out. The Gosmaire's were not in agreement. Andy asked for 10 to 15 years with probation. The McBrides concurred. Conor said his fate was in the parents' hands.

It took Jack Campbell several weeks to come back with his plea recommendation: 25 years straight or 20 years with 10 years of probation. Conor chose the latter. Campbell's recommendation counted more than anyone else's, and he prevailed.

Today, Connor is at Wakulla Correctional Institution, which is just 30 miles south of where the Gosmaire's live. He has a job as a clerk in the law library. He calls her parents every Tuesday, and they go to see him about four times a year. As part of his sentence and eventual probation, Conor also has to take anger management classes in prison. He has to speak to people about teen dating violence. And when he gets out, he has to do community service. To honor Ann, he plans on volunteering at the animal shelter or a wildlife refuge.

Kate Gosmaire recently said, "Ours is a story of radical forgiveness. I'm a sane human today because of it. And people who have heard our story have been able to forgive others. I'm not expecting anybody to forgive anything as big as I have. But it's encouraging to see it when it happens."

## Ebrahim Mohebi: January 2, 2009, 6 AM

This true story comes from *Salt Lake Tribune, Mercy vs. Grief: Father Must Make Life-or-Death Call in Iran Revolution*, Monday, February 7, 2009

Islamic law holds to the dictum of eye-for-eye, tooth-for-tooth, and life-for-life. A grim example occurred in Iran when a young boy named Hamed violated the newly enforced law which made it a legal sin to break the fast during Ramadan by smoking. He was seen and challenged by a Basiji—enforcer of religious laws—a twenty-four-year-old named Shahid Mohebi. Hamed refused to cooperate and left the area in anger only to return shortly and to start a fight with Shahid, the Basiji. The fight became violent, and a seventeen-year-old hothead, named Morteza Amimi Moqaddam, slashed and stabbed Shahid multiple times resulting in the young Basiji's death before multiple witnesses. It was December 11, 2008

Moreza was tried in Sharia court, convicted, and sentenced to death by hanging as prescribed by Qur'anic law. At six a.m. on January 2, 2009. Under Sharia law, the murder victim's father, Ebrahim Mohebi, had the right to overturn the Sharia council's verdict and to set the murderer of his son free from the fear of hanging for the rest of his life. Not only was it a heavy moral burden, but it had become a nation-wide major political struggle between conservatives and more liberals of the country. Either way Ebrahim chose could spark a massive riot in a country sensitive to power struggles, especially when a religious issue was involved.

On the one hand, by law, the murderer of his son, who stood only a few feet from Ebrahim, could pay the ultimate price—death by hanging then and there. Or, as a true and life-long Muslim, and a lover of peace, Ebrahim could—by a few words—free the killer from the death sentence and thereby to incur the wrath of the true believers in the revolution, and might risk being beaten to death by an enraged mob of conservative zealots.

He stood in silence and pondered the quandary. The crowd became silent as well, aware of Ebrahim's torment. Finally, he spoke, and in a voice that could be heard by all present, said, "God gives life, and God takes it. I will forget about this sin against me so that God will forgive our sins."

Morteza Amimi Moqaddam was saved from hanging by Ebrahim's profound act of love. He was led away back to prison to stand for another punishment trial that would not be able to impose capital punishment.

## Samareh Ali Nezhad [Alinejad] and Abdolqani Hossein Zadeh: Wednesday, early morning April 15, 2014:

On December 21, 2007, Abdollah Hosseinzadeh, age 17, and 19-year-old Bilal Abdullah met in a Wednesday street bazaar in Nour–located in the northern province of Mazandaran, 143 miles from Tehran. As witnessed, and testified to, by street vendor onlookers, Abdollah was taking a stroll in the bazaar with his friends when Bilal shoved him. Abdollah took offense and kicked Bilal. The older boy took an ordinary kitchen knife out of his socks and stabbed Abdollah, who bled to death. Bilal was arrested by police after fleeing the crime scene.

Bilal was tried and sentenced to death by hanging, pending appeals. Abdollah's parents who suffered the death of their younger son, 11 year-old Amir, in 2003 when he was run over while riding his bicycle by a motorcycle. Bilal was a passenger on that motorcycle. They were doubly grief-stricken when Abdollah was murdered and also enraged. They insisted throughout the appeals process that Bilal be hanged in retribution. The retaliation law in Iran [an eye for eye and life for life] allows—even requires–the murder victim's family to have active involvement in the punishment process. They must either seek revenge from the murderer or spare his/her life—their choice.

Technically under patriarchal Islamic and Iran's Sharia law, the father has the right and duty to make the decision. Mother Samareh was so absolutely inflexible in favor of the execution of the man who robbed her of her son, that Father Abdolqani relinquished that role to his wife. After seven years, the appeals process was exhausted; and public execution was scheduled.

The day before the execution, a high-profile campaign was launched by ISNA [Iranian Students News Agency] with public figures including Adel Ferdosipour, a popular football commentator and TV show host, and former international footballer Ali Daei. They made a strenuous appeal for the victim's family to forgive the killer. The host of a popular live show 90 called the couple and pled with them to spare the convict's life. Samareh resisted all pressure and remained adamant that she was going to be the final instrument in a hanging.

"We couldn't sleep that night; we were all awake until morning. Until the last minute, I didn't want to forgive. "I had told my husband just two days before that I can't forgive this man, but maybe there would be a possibility, but I couldn't persuade myself to forgive." Samareh said.

"My husband said, 'look to God and let's see what happens…' You have the final say, my husband had said," she recalled. "He said you've suffered too much, we'll do as you say."

90 is a show about soccer, with an impressive viewer rate of approximately 30 million; so, a large divide was created between the pro-hanging Muslims and the anti-hanging believers. They exerted great pressure on Samareh. By that day, Bilal's mother had given up hope that he might be spared.

Mother Samareh responded questions forced on her by asking, "Do you how difficult it is to live in an empty house? Do you understand that my life became like poison?"

She was furious at the injustice of being a mother having to suffer another great loss.

During the night before the scheduled hanging, Samareh reported a vivid dream. in which her son came to her, asking her not to take revenge.

"Two nights before that day," she said, "I saw him in the dream once again, but this time he refused to speak to me."

Between four a.m. and six a.m. on the day of the execution, hundreds of Iranians gathered at the execution site; some to cheer it on; some to shout for mercy for Bilal; and many just excited onlookers. 26-year-old Bilal was dragged from the prison doors by burly prison guards struggling and screaming. The crowd began to chant.

The simple gallows was ready in the street for Bilal. It consisted of an overhead trestle and a wooden four-legged chair with a back for the condemned to stand on. Bilal struggled, screamed, and prayed loudly, as he was bound and forced to stand on the chair. After a recitation from the Qur'an was read, the guards placed the heavy gallows rope around his neck. There were mere seconds before he drew his last breath.

Abdollah's parents strode purposefully to the gallows and walked directly up to where Bilal was standing, blindfolded.

Many in the crowd began shouting "Forgive him, forgive him."

Others cried, "Amoo Ghani [uncle Ghani], forgive," calling the victim's father by his first name.

They were—along with Bilal's mother—asking the family of the victim to pardon their young son. They were suffering from the drama of the spectacle and knowing its climax. He was screaming and praying loudly before he just went silent. Despite being blindfolded by a black hood, he became aware of the Hosseinzadeh family's presence and began to address them by their familiar names, begging.

The blindfolded Bilal, weeping, begged Samareh one last time.

"Forgive me, Aunt Maryam," he pleaded, addressing her by the nickname by which she was widely known in the community. "Show your mercy."

Samareh moved in close and given a chair to stand on to be able see him face to face. The crowd watched for her foot to kick the chair out from under him and to bring about the judicial hanging.

"Did you have mercy on us? Did you show mercy to my son?" she demanded. "You have taken happiness away from us. Why should I have mercy toward you?"

Samareh stared angrily at him. The next second's pause was an eternity. Then, she slapped him hard across the face. She and her husband slipped the noose off his neck, and with that move, Bilal's death sentence had been commuted. Some in the crowd applauded. Others stood silently shocked. When Bilal stepped down from the chair, Samareh kicked it away.

Bilal's mother Kobra, sobbing, reached across the fence separating the crowd from the execution site, and embraced Samareh before reaching to kiss her feet–a gesture of profound respect and gratitude. Samareh did not allow her to do that. She took Kobra's arm and made her stand up. Later she told reports why: "she was just a mother like me, after all."

The two mothers embraced and sobbed in each other's arms.

"After that," she recalled, "I felt as if rage had vanished within my heart. I felt as if the blood in my veins began to flow again. "I felt at ease and forgave him," she said. "I burst into tears and called my husband up to remove the noose."

Seven years after the murder, the victim's family had spared the life of the murderer at the gallows. They currently live quietly in Iran's northern Mazandaran province on the Caspian Sea, with their daughter, their now only remaining child. Abdolqani Hossein Zadeh–Abdollah's father–is a former soccer player of local teams and currently active as the principal of the Nour City Soccer Academy. He decided to use the court-ordered 115,000 USD blood money to which he was entitled, to found a soccer academy in the name of his son. The young convict whose life was spared was required to spend the next 12 years in prison, with credit for the seven-years-time served. The Hosseinzadeh family gave him a fresh start.

Iran has the second highest number of executions in the world–369 in 2013–after China, according to Amnesty International. The practice known as Qisas in Iran was displayed that week in 2017 when the family of a young man murdered in a street fight prepared to hang his killer in public by pushing away the chair he stood on at the gallows.

The heir to the person murdered [the walli-ye-dam] may–with the permission of the hakim-i-shar' [judge]–execute the Qisas personally, or may appoint his agent for this purpose, according to a translation of the Iran's Islamic Penal Code. Qisas literally equates the punishment with the crime, allowing victims to punish their attackers in manners other than execution. In 2011, for example, an Iranian woman blinded by a man she spurned opted to enact revenge by having him blinded, as well.

In the next sentence on Qisas, however, it adds: "It is better to forgive." Taking this advice to heart, one Iranian mother–Samareh Ali Nezhad [Alinejad]–made global headlines after forgiving her son's murderer at the last moment, thereby enshrining herself as a hero.

Harsh Iranian laws have been attacked outside Iran as a violation of human rights. But Iran still defends its practice of Qisas.

"As I've said before, many of the issues raised on the pretext of human rights, including opposing the death penalty, are in fact in opposition to Islam, because *Qisas* [retribution] is clearly stipulated in the *Qur'an*," the head of Iran's Judiciary Ayatollah Sadegh Larijani said in late 2013.

## Martin "Marty" Hartigan 2019:

Marty was twenty-one years old when he graduated from Stanford. He was already a success having been a star athlete on the rugby team. He was employed as a Deloitte consultant and enjoying the fruits of his fine education and high work ethic. There was one element of his life that was less than fully enjoyable: he had to work away from his home in Coto de Caza, California in Chicago during the week and fly back every Sunday night on the red-eye. He kept an apartment in the windy city; and, on Monday, July 16, 2019, he had a client meeting. He got through it, but felt ill, unusually tired. He developed chills and had to steel himself to prevent shaking. He presumed it was the flu, and he would be all right in a couple of days. After all, he was a very fit 185-pound former rugby player with an excellent immune system. It was a nuisance, but not a worry.

He stayed in his apartment, resting, drinking Gatorade, and taking Tylenol without getting any better. The next morning, Tuesday, July

17, 2019, his daughter, Kayleigh—who, at the time was a junior at the University of Virginia in Charlottesville–who happened to be visiting on a layover, noticed that her father was struggling to talk. Aware that this was certainly more than a flu, Kayleigh refused to leave for the airport until he at least saw a doctor. She looked up the closest emergency room on the internet, then called an Uber to go to Northwestern Memorial Hospital. Marty was wearing flip-flops, shorts, and his Winston Churchill "We Shall Never Surrender" T-shirt. He was unable even to stand during their elevator ride down from the 35th floor of his building. When he arrived at the ER with Kayleigh, he remembers someone asking if he had a do-not-resuscitate order.

His answer was, "No! I want to be resuscitated!" and it was emphatic.

Then, he said, "I blacked out for 10 days."

In the ER, he was intubated and placed on a ventilator. When Darcy arrived in Chicago to be with her husband, she was amazed at all the life-support machines he had to have.

Physicians repeatedly delivered dire prognoses: "Every time a doctor walked in the room, my heart would constrict," Darcey said. "I really hated when the doctors came in the room."

When he regained consciousness, Hartigan learned he had had a very near-death experience for ten days. A strep A bacterial infection– possibly from strep throat–and his body's unusually strong inflammatory response to it, had dramatically lowered his blood pressure, causing septic shock and multiorgan failure. A rare hyperclotting condition–purpura fulminans–led to blocked arteries throughout his body.

The medical/surgical crew faced daunting decisions: Ensuring that enough blood and oxygen flowed to Hartigan's heart and brain—the priority for life—meant not enough could get to his extremities. So, when he regained consciousness, Marty saw that his limbs were "shriveled and dark—like, brown," he said. Surgeons amputated both legs from just below the knee, then his left arm below his elbow, and the right thumb, index finger, fifth, and middle fingers down to the last joint two weeks later—most of his remaining hand. Some of the operations took eight to 10 hours. Over nearly three months, Hartigan had 18 surgeries, many of them to remove dead tissue to preserve his knees with an eye toward his future mobility.

Clara Schroedl–the assistant professor of medicine and medical education at Northwestern University who was Hartigan's critical-care doctor during the first few days—said, "Anyone who needs the intensive care unit could die… within our intensive care unit, we have severity of illness that varies… [and] He was way on the side of severe."

Marty entered Northwestern University Hospital in mid-July, had four near death experiences, had to have multiple amputations, and was finally released in November and moved to nearby Shirley Ryan AbilityLab. Instead of giving in to the disaster of losing his limbs and very nearly his life, Marty cheerfully worked daily for six weeks with physical and occupational therapists to regain strength and to learn how to slide out of bed into a wheelchair—both arduously won accomplishments. Then he moved back to his Chicago apartment, returning to AbilityLab twice a week for three hours of PT and OT.

The staff nicknamed him "Marty Harty"—a play on *hardy* and *hearty*.

In January, Eileen Wilmsen, Hartigan's occupational therapist at AbilityLab was helping Hartigan figure out new ways to perform everyday tasks: how to shave, toast a bagel and spread it with cream cheese, take a shower, eat independently and transfer from his wheelchair to the toilet. Hartigan calls them "things you take for granted." By February, he and Wilmsen were working on "life hacks," such as using a tongue depressor to pop open the lids of food-storage containers. Reusable storage bags proved trickier. "Ziploc is like Kryptonite to me," Hartigan said. He looked around: "What's next? What can I open next?"

"He's really had a great attitude about the whole thing and a lot of gratitude," observed Mark Huang, an AbilityLab physician and a professor in the department of physical medicine and rehabilitation at Northwestern University's Feinberg School of Medicine. "It's a long road."

Instead of bemoaning his losses, the pain, and the fear for what the rest of his life might be, Marty chose to be grateful for what was saved, "It's much easier to learn to walk on prosthetics where you have your knee," he said.

"Marty is and was the best patient ever. Life is short. These terrible things can happen. No matter what ridiculous decision we had to make, he always remained positive," Jason Ko, Marty's plastic surgeon, said of him.

He did have a low point, by his own admission: he broke a tooth on a Subway flatbread chicken sandwich in October. "I was despondent," he said. "I couldn't believe that after everything else, my tooth cracked. I had a pity party for about a half hour."

A year after his near-death experience, and the hardest work of his life, the former Stanford rugby player who ran 1,000 miles in 2018—the year before his illness—has had to come to terms with a different life and body.

"Life as a quad amputee is the new normal," Hartigan said, looking realistically at his fate.

His former life was—by all accounts—a picture perfect Hallmark holiday card one. He was a partner at one of the world's top consulting firms and lived in a beautiful Southern California house with a home gym. He had married his sweetheart from his UCLA business-school days, Darcey, who taught high school until the arrival of their second child, Matt, now a sophomore at Indiana University. Despite the separations from Darcy due to work requirements–like traveling to meet clients in Illinois, Texas, and Mississippi–he still managed to coach Little League for Matt. All in all, life was good then.

He had been a fit 185 pounds before he entered the hospital; he weighed just 125 pounds four months later. With a surfeit of work and grit, Marty is now back up to 165 pounds. Given that he is minus an estimated 20 pounds for the amputated limbs, he is again the full Marty. The remarkable thing about Marty Hartigan—besides the fact that he is alive—is that he has retained his cheerful personality throughout the entire ordeal.

Hartigan's hospitalization and, nine months later, the pandemic shutdown, combined to change all the Hallmark life. The family spent the following spring huddled in Hartigan's two-room Chicago apartment, with rehab and Keyleigh's college on pause. Marty–whose skin was still healing and who couldn't be bumped during the night–slept in the smaller room, and Matt, Kayleigh, and Darcey, slept in the other. They fashioned a desk for Matt by duct-taping a closet door to two barstools.

Finally, Marty and Darcey returned to Southern California. The house in Coto de Caza did not work. In late 2019, they sold their 4,500-square-foot house—too big for empty nesters and not wheelchair friendly. And in

April, they bought a one-story home in San Clemente, California that they are retrofitting with an accessible bathroom and wider doorways—part of the new normal.

Keyleigh has inherited her father's upbeat outlook: "It's like a second chance, we appreciate the things we didn't appreciate before, like being together."

Little things are much more fully appreciated, like going to the bathroom, in Marty's case. He spent a few unhappy weeks on dialysis before his kidneys miraculously started to work again. Or making a peanut butter and jelly sandwich with his hook hand. He needed help to learn how to figure out new ways to perform everyday tasks–how to shave, toast a bagel and spread it with cream cheese, neatly fold laundry, take a shower, eat independently, and transfer from his wheelchair to the toilet. He typically texts and types by dictating to speech-recognition software, then correcting its mistakes with the remaining joint of his right middle finger.

Hartigan calls them "things you take for granted."

"I started to tell people I was the king of pee," says Hartigan. "I never got upset. I never went through the 'Why me?'"

He never lost his optimism for life nor his infectious self-deprecating humor.

In physical therapy, Laura Vinci de Vanegas had Hartigan balance on a big medicine ball.

"If I fell forward, I'd fall on my face," Hartigan said afterward. "I was nervous, but I just kind of went for it."

Then he did it again, face plant and all.

"Marty, you'll be teaching adaptive Pilates!" Laura exclaimed.

She emphasized repeatedly that this work–and soon, prosthetic legs–would help Marty return to life in the community. He keeps at it even today.

Fritz Glaser–an orthopedic surgeon in Fresno, California–and a Sigma Chi brother of Hartigan's, jumped in to serve as Hartigan's medical interpreter and advocate during his four-month hospital stay, and later "MacGyvered" an easy wheelchair-to-toilet seat, a shower chair, and a shower head with a hose, for his Chicago apartment. Marty has acquired a special van with a hydraulic lift to be able to get around. The two friends were each other's best men at their respective weddings.

"He's the most loyal human being I've ever met," Hartigan says.

Hartigan's doctors told him to assume he is at high risk of COVID-19 complications; so, he had to stop going to outpatient PT and OT temporarily. Darcey felt safe running outdoors. Not Kayleigh, who worried she'd contract COVID-19 and infect her dad. The COVID pandemic was another hill for climbers in the Hartigan family.

On June 3, it was finally time. Hartigan took a COVID test and was readmitted to AbilityLab. The next day, he took his new, custom prosthetic legs for a hobble around the lab, using a walker. The day after that, he walked about 40 feet. Back in California after July, Hartigan uses the prosthetics and walker rather than a wheelchair when he leaves the house. Doctors expect that someday he will be able to run again.

Hartigan was motivated by an additional goal, "I want to be taller than my son again," he said in the spring.

Matt is 5-foot-11, and Hartigan had a half inch on him before his amputations. He may realize his goal as the prosthetics are adjusted. There is always hope.

Regardless of who is taller at any given moment, Matt still looks up to his father. For Christmas, Matt gave his father silver dog tags that read, "To my dad. I'll always be your little boy. You'll always be my hero!" Hartigan always wears them.

Hartigan works on both his mind and body to focus on near-term goals.

"I don't think about it being like one gigantic milestone," he says. [I work on] "being patient in all ways, being patient when things are hard to do."

In the new normal, Marty took a yearlong medical leave of absence and then retired from Deloitte. At present he does not know whether he will be able to return to full-time work. For the time being, he will continue to work on rebooting.

"Marty being who he was–the primary guy everybody turned to in tough times–made all of us feel we had to be twice as supportive," says old rugby teammate Sean Walters. For their 30th reunion weekend, Tim Brien, visited Hartigan in Chicago instead of heading to the Stanford campus. Two Sigma Chi brothers came along.

Brien sees a parallel between Hartigan's situation and poker, which the Sigma Chis always used to play together, "Just because you're dealt a bad hand doesn't mean you're out of the game. You can still win with a bad hand."

## Bridger Walker [b. 2014], Summer, 2020

Bridger was born in Cheyenne, Wyoming in 2014 to an ordinary middle-class family. He was the third child. His father, Robert, was a lawyer; and his mother, Teila, ran the house and cared for the growing children. At the time, Bridger had an elder brother and an older sister. The children's names are withheld in the interests of the parents' desire for privacy. Bridger's aunt, Nicole Noel "Nikki, sometimes "Aunt Cole", Walker, and her supportive husband were frequent fixtures in the family. The family might well have been the quintessential American family.

The family waited expectantly for the arrival of a new, fourth, member of the family. Robert, Teila, and Nikki, had some concerns about how Bridger would react to the new child, since she might take his place as the favored youngest of the clan. Any fears they had were immediately dispelled when Bridger met new "Little Sister", Brielle, on the day of her birth. His "world was rocked" his aunt said.

Without hesitation, he jumped into the oversized hospital chair and waited patiently for his turn to hold her.

His mother said of him, "Since that moment, it was clear to us that there was a special bond between him and his sister."

Everyone in the family agrees that–from that moment–Bridger "rarely strays far from his little sister" and describes him as, "gregarious, always learning, so full of love and an absolute joy to have in our lives". Maybe something a bit more than ordinary.

The ordinariness changed on a fateful day in the summer of 2016 when 6-year-old Bridger took the hand of his "Little Sister", 4-year-old Brielle—a delicate little blond, and walked to the house of some neighborhood friends to play with their dog—with the consent of both sets of parents. The two Walker children knocked politely at the neighbor's door. The girl who let them in was Bridger's age.

As soon as they were in the house, she gave them a warning. There were two dogs, she said, a nice one they could play with; and a mean one they had to stay away from. They walked through the house to the back yard. When they were just outside the patio door, the neighbor child with them pointed to one dog and said "that is the nice dog," and pointed to the other dog in the yard, explaining, "this is the mean one." The "mean" dog–a year-old German Shepard–mix immediately charged at "Little Sister", growling and vicious.

Without even the slightest hesitation, Bridger leaped to put himself between the snarling attacking dog and his beloved little sister. The snapping dog grabbed the young boy, clamping his teeth and jaws down on the left side of Bridger's face and mauled him. With the dog's jaws still clamped on his face, Bridger grabbed Brielle's hand and pulled her to a more secure part of the yard where he thought they would be safe.

Bridger said, "I stepped to the side, in front of my sister so that the dog wouldn't get her; I kept moving; so, it couldn't get past."

The owner secured the dog and ran to Bridger's aid, applying pressure to his wound and called for urgent medical care.

His personal risk of even being killed by the relentless dog was something Bridger understood. He ignored that as well. What was important to him was that his little sister be saved.

"Little Sister" was saved from any physical harm. Bridger's courageous action unfortunately resulted in the dog slashing a jagged open wound on his face, and he received an unsightly scar on his face which ruined the quality of his warm and charming smile.

Following the attack, Bridger was taken to the Cheyenne Regional Medical Center. There he underwent a two-hour surgery requiring 90 sutures by Dr. Joseph F. Looby, a plastic surgeon. Dr. Looby told the family that they would have to wait as long as two years to be able to do additional surgery to correct the disfigurement, which was disheartening. In accordance with his newly identified extraordinariness, Bridger's spirit was not deterred. He did not even see himself as anything special. However, his parents were not really surprised that their son had behaved as a hero for his sister.

"To Us, it was a miracle when Bridger was born as our third child."

It was part of his character. Bridger himself said, that he was proud of his scar, because it meant he helped his little sister. His father, Robert, told *People Magazine* that Bridger "views his scar as something to be proud of. My wife and I asked him, 'Do you want it to go away?' And he said, 'I don't want it to go all the way away'... Bridger views his scar as something to be proud of, but he also doesn't see it as being representative of his brave act. He just perceives it as, 'I was a brother and that's what brothers do.' It's a reminder that his sister didn't get hurt, and that she is okay."

After Bridger and his parents arrived at the hospital, an animal control officer arrived to let the family know that the dog–a 1-year-old German Shepherd mix–was up to date on vaccinations, as well as that the owners had made the decision to have the dog "euthanized".

When Bridger Walker to protect his younger sister from being attacked, the world praised him as a hero. His willingness to sacrifice himself to protect his younger sister made headlines around the world, and Bridger was hailed as a hero for his bravery and courage. His family permitted courteous interviews with Bridger but has protected him from the media storm generally. In more than one interview, the shy and direct boy simply reasoned his actions with, "If someone had to die, I thought it should be me." Even a year later, Bridger's father, Robert Walker; his son still stood by those words.

There was a remarkable amount of media hoopla and genuinely expressed congratulations and affection by a loving press, movie stars, friends, and neighbors. That did not change the strong efforts by Robert and Teila to keep their children's lives normal and average. Bridger has had two dogs, a German Shepherd/ Collie cross named Elektra, and a Poodle/ Lab cross named Thor. Sadly, Elektra died of old age in November, 2020.

Mrs. Walker said, "We are very thankful that we still have Thor around to keep us helping Bridger and his siblings to heal from Bridger's incident... We've been doing the balancing act of normal family life with focusing on Bridger's recovery."

The enthusiasm of the media and the general public has scarcely dimmed through the years to the time of this writing in 2023. The local Cheyenne newspaper reported, "Cheyenne's own hero, Bridger Walker, was appointed "Honorary Champion" and named "Bravest Man in the World" by the World Boxing Council in 2020. The high honor by the WBC recognized Bridger's bravery during a dog attack in July 2020. In honor of his heroic actions, the WBC created a new boxing weight class called "The Bridgerweight" to memorialize his deeds." The honor came in the WBC 60th Annual Convention in Acapulco, Mexico. In another edition, a headline read, **"Bridger Walker Passes the Baton to a New 'Hero of Humanity, Dunia Sibomara'."**

Bridger Walker met Dunia Sibomara, a fourteen-year-old boy from the Congo who survived a chimpanzee attack at the age of six. Sibomara underwent several surgeries for his injuries in the United States. In 2022, Sibomara was adopted by Long Beach Middle School wrestling coach Miguel Rodriguez. Three weeks later, he went on to win the 102-pound New York State wrestling title.

In an emotionally charged ceremony, Bridger Walker greeted his fellow "Hero of Humanity" and honored Dunia by awarding him with the green and gold WBC belt. British Boxing News reported that the two boys became friends, enjoying a week of swimming, playing around the hotel, and "enjoying every moment" of their stay. According to an interview with WBC, Dunia has been showing Bridger the ropes of wrestling. According to Dunia, Bridger "caught onto it really quick." The two went zip-lining together with Bridger's family; Dunia said that was the best part of his trip. The newspaper editorialized: "It sounds like the two will be friends for years to come."

When the public learned via social media and news outlets that Bridger was an enthusiastic rock hound, mail trucks full of rocks began to arrive at the Walker's address. People were sending rocks–tens of thousands of rocks, stories of rocks, pictures of rocks. Some people sent other items that carried sentimental value: like an honorary green beret someone sent him in recognition of his bravery. Another man mailed Bridger his Purple Heart.

The University of Wyoming Geological Museum opened an exhibit of some of his rocks on November 12. In introducing his son's exhibit that night at the opening reception, Robert said the collection is less about Bridger's heroism than it is about the kindness and support people have shown a little boy.

Robert said of his son that, "It's amazing; the wonderful, miraculous support Bridger has received from around the world," Robert said. "I don't know what his emotional recovery would have been without it. It took his mind off his recovery. His wound would drip, but instead of worrying about the drops of blood all over his shirt, he always had the next package to look forward to… and he never got an inflated head."

Over the years—alongside his father and older brother—Bridger has trained in Brazilian jiu jitsu; and by being one of the youngest and smallest in the class, he has always been up against larger and more experienced opponents.

News reports that Bridger would have to wait one or even two years to begin definitive surgical repair of his wounds received sympathy from all over the world. However, New York City-based Dr. Dhaval Bhanusali reached out to the family to offer his services and explained how new technology could allow immediate treatment with better results.

"Dr. Bhanusali gave us hope that everything would be alright and that we could make real progress in a few months rather than a few years," Robert Walker said. "After going above and beyond to provide support, encouragement, and expert care, he reinforced our appreciation for the life-altering care that dermatologists provide."

The Walker family traveled to New York, where Bridger received the first in a series of scar treatments. In addition to Bhanusali, the Walker family has also been working with Utah-based dermatologist Cory Maughan for Bridger's scar treatments.

"While the world and I celebrated Bridger's incredible heroism and bravery, I also thought about how the scars from this attack could affect him physically, mentally, and emotionally," Bhanusali said. "Working with Bridger and his family has been so rewarding, and I'm grateful to collaborate with Dr. Maughan so that Bridger can continue his care closer to home."

"Despite being across the country, Dr. Bhanusali and I are working together closely to ensure Bridger gets the best treatment possible and that he and his family are comfortable with his care," said Dr. Maughan. "After everything Bridger and his family have been through, we want to give him every opportunity for his scars to look their best."

Bridger's smile is improving dramatically. Through it all, Bridger has remained an ordinary extraordinary boy and has not developed an "inflated head."

## Three Female Fighters:

11-Year-Old Girl [unnamed due to her age]—Escambia County, Florida, May 19, 2021; Cherokee Brodersen Salt Lake City, Utah on Monday, June 6, 2022; 8-year-old girl [unnamed due to her age], Whittier Elementary School, West Valley City, Utah, Thursday, April 6, 2023:

## 11-year-old girl hero

On Tuesday morning, May 19, 2021, 7 a.m., an 11-year-old girl in Escambia County, Florida fought off a man who tried to kidnap her from a bus stop in a harrowing incident caught on video. Escambia County is the westernmost and oldest county in the State of Florida. It is in the state's north-western corner. It is the county seat and largest city is Pensacola, population, 321,905.

The young girl fought and kept fighting and never gave up. She screamed, yelled, kicked, and punched, her would-be kidnapper during his criminal attempt.

"Had this 11-year-old victim not thought to fight and to fight and to just never give up, then this could have ended terribly," Escambia County Sheriff Chip W. Simmons said. "We have caught the animal that tried to kidnap an 11-year-old girl this morning," the Sheriff said announcing the arrest.

The 11-year-old girl was waiting for the bus and playing with some blue slime as she sat in a grassy area near the road. A white van can be seen in surveillance footage released by the sheriff's department pulling up alongside the girl. A man jumped out and approached her with a knife in his hand. He picked the slight girl up and attempted to carry her to the van. The girl was able to fight back and escape before the man ran back to the van and quickly drove away.

"She fought, and she fought, and she fought, until finally she was able to break free from her would be captor," Sheriff Simmons said of the heroic escape.

The plucky girl reported the kidnapping attempt to her parents, who called the Escambia County Sheriff's Office, which launched an immediate massive manhunt for the suspect. The sheriff's office deployed at least 50 deputies and plain clothes detectives to knock on doors in the area and obtain surveillance footage that helped them identify the vehicle and license plate used in the alleged attack.

Armed with that information, investigators were able to track Jared Paul Stanga to his home later that same day, where they found the van had been freshly painted in an attempt to disguise the vehicle. Jared Stanga, 30, now faces charges of attempted kidnapping of a child under 13, and aggravated assault and battery. Authorities were able to link him to the crime through surveillance footage that captured the vehicle used in the kidnapping attempt.

Investigators also said they obtained pictures from a convenience store that showed Stanga wearing the same clothes that the attempted kidnapper had been wearing in the surveillance footage and said he had "blue slime over his own arms" that matched the slime the young girl had been playing with when she was attacked. He was arrested without incident.

The young girl told authorities that the same man had approached her about two weeks ago and "made her feel uncomfortable," Sheriff Simmons said.

The 11-year-old had told her parents, teachers, and principal, about that encounter; but the sheriff said he did not believe law enforcement had been called at the time.

"I am very proud of the efforts of the Escambia County Sheriff's Office, but I cannot help to think that this could have ended very differently," Simmons said. "Had this 11-year-old victim not thought to fight and to fight and to just never give up, then this could have ended terribly."

Simmons said the suspect had an "extensive criminal history" that included sexual offenses with a child.

"This man needs to be off the streets," Simmons said.

The girl suffered some scratches and is still dealing with the emotional trauma of the experience but is expected to be okay.

"My message to her is that she's my hero," Simmons said. "My message is that she did not give up, she did the right thing, she fought, and she fought, and she fought; and she never gave up."

Amen, brother, amen to every word of that!

Cherokee—originally from Naples, Florida–lived in the area of 800 South and 500 East streets in Salt Lake City, Utah. According to acquaintances, she was employed at Blue Grass-hopper Brewery and Pub in Rio Rancho, Artesian Well Park–a small urban park in downtown Salt Lake City that contains a natural artesian spring fed by an underground aquifer. It occupies a quarter acre on the southwest corner of the intersection between 800 South and 500 East. People from all over the surrounding area have been coming to get water for free from this spring for over 100 years.

Ms. Brodersen was walking to meet a friend in the area where she lived on Monday, July 6, 2022 at ~11:30 p.m. EDT, to go see a friend play music at a nearby bar. Roughly two blocks away from her home, Cherokee was approached by a man who initially seemed like he was going to flirt with her. According to Cherokee's sister, Charidy, the man was about five-foot-seven and looked anywhere from 26 to 30-years-old. He had sandy, coarse, shorter blonde hair, with shadow-like facial hair.

The man had leg tattoos and was driving what the sisters think was a maroon or teal Sedan. The Brodersens' noted that the suspect was good looking and both well-kept and spoken.

When he first addressed Cherokee, the man said, "Let's go out. Come with me. Let's go have a good time."

Cherokee denied the man multiple times and explained that she was headed to meet a friend. From there, Charidy said the man stood in front of her sister, brandished a gun from under his shirt, and ordered her to get in his car.

"He had his gun right here (pointing to my chest), and he was like, 'Get in the car, b—,' I said, 'You're going to have to shoot me right now because I'm not getting into your car.'"

"My sister told him he was going to have to shoot her in the street before she would get in his car," said Charidy.

The man then fired his weapon into the air and began to wrestle with Brodersen. The middle-aged woman was pistol whipped in the face several times as a result. According to Charidy, her sister "fought so hard!"

She fell but kept screaming. Ms. Brodersen–who was in a walking boot at the time–said, that she soon figured out the man was not going to take "no" for an answer. She said the man fired a shot in the air and a struggle ensued, with the man trying to push Brodersen back toward his car, which was running with a door open.

"He hit me behind the ear with the gun, and I felt my knees go; when I got back up, he punched me in the face with the gun and started pulling me down the sidewalk by my hair."

Brodersen was relentless despite her injury and pain. After lingering for several seconds, the attacker finally had enough and ran off, leaving Brodersen slumped on the sidewalk. She was relieved that she was alive. Surveillance video captured the gun shot and Cherokee's screams, which appeared to be effective in finally causing the attacker to run.

"I don't know what the plan was; but I was like, I would rather be shot on the sidewalk than delay it," she said.

Ms. Brodersen said she suffered multiple fractures to her jaw, face and around her eye socket. Her eye showed deep bruising around it on Wednesday evening. Cherokee said she needs surgery on her face.

Not only did the attack take a toll physically; it also affected her psyche.

"Walking around in the dark is never going to feel the same," Brodersen said, turning emotional. "I don't know if he's trying to find me or what. I think he's just gonna do it again, because he didn't get what he wanted," Ms. Brodersen said.

Due to the incident, Cherokee has suffered a concussion and several broken bones in her face which called for a four-hour facial reconstruction surgery with a plate. Charidy said that the medical bills are piling up at a time when Cherokee's injuries have put her out of work.

## Utah Third Grader, April 6, 2023:

An 8-year-old third grader at Whittier Elementary School in Granite School District in West Valley City fought off an attempted kidnapping on Thursday, April 6, 2023. The unnamed child was attacked at 3: 50 p.m. after school. The attack was caught on surveillance video. The girl had already walked to her mother's car–parked at the nearby Hunter Park pick-up and drop-off area. She was waiting with her mother for an older sister after class. The mother asked her daughter to go to the front of the building to make sure the older sibling knew they were waiting in the back of the school.

The would-be kidnapper walked up to her on a pathway outside the north side of the school. She tried to get around him because she could tell something was not right, the video showed; and the man talked to her briefly. Then he quickly reached out to give her a hug and grabbed her. The video then showed the man dragging the girl around a corner into an alcove that was ~30 to 40 feet long.

She screamed, kicked, and hit, the man, furiously and relentlessly. School employees eventually heard her cries for help and approached. The little girl fought herself free as a school employee–who was watching students as they crossed 6000 West–heard her cries and rushed over to her. According to police, the intended kidnapper ran toward 6000 West and turned north toward 3500 South. The suspect was described as light-skinned, between 5 feet 9 inches and 5 feet 11 inches tall and 150-160 pounds. He was wearing a black striped beanie, a blue and gray sweatshirt with the California state flag on it, gray sweatpants, and a black backpack at the time of the attempted kidnapping, as seen in surveillance photos released by the school district. The young man was suspected of being homeless.

The young victim was not physically harmed in the incident. "Considering the nature of the attack, she is doing quite well," school officials said.

Investigators announced Saturday night that a 16-year-old boy had been detained in relation to the incident. He was a student in a "non-traditional" program in the school district and lived near the elementary school. Granite School District Police Chief Randy Porter said Friday that the man could face charges of attempted kidnapping and assault.

The school district said Friday that it will staff additional officers–from its own police department and West Valley City's–around the school and other district facilities while it investigates. The district spokesman expressed concern about the brazen nature of the attack and feared that he or other individuals might seek to attack at Whittier School again or at other locations.

The three possible kidnapping victims were by any criteria, heroes. Not only did they fight their attackers until they broke free, but they never stopped until they were free. There is a strong lesson there: Start teaching children and women about stranger danger and about the idea that fighting back and screaming is good and acceptable practice. No adult has the slightest right to manhandle a girl or a woman, or anyone, for that matter. Assault, battery, and kidnapping, are crimes; and attackers deserve the full wrath of the law and to be taken off the streets. It is irrelevant what their personal circumstances are: the child or the woman is the victim, and the attacker is the perpetrator. Period. They have no business being part of free society for a long time.

The present author taught self-defense/Jiu Jitsu classes to women and girls. The lessons included techniques for fighting, but more importantly stressed the two best defenses: 1) Run away. 2) If that fails, scream, yell, kick, head butt, punch with flailing fists, scratch eyes, squeeze parts, bite—whatever it takes. Do not give up. Perps are usually cowards. Never, never, allow yourself to be dragged into a car or van. Almost always, disaster awaits inside that vehicle. It is better to die on the sidewalk than to endure the fate that lies in the vehicle.

Parents and teachers, ensure that every child is in the company of trusted people at all times. Women and children, do not go out anywhere, anytime, alone at night, no matter how safe you think the area is or how tough you think you are. Prevention beats cure every time.


–THE END–

www.ingramcontent.com/pod-product-compliance
Lightning Source LLC
Chambersburg PA
CBHW052057090426
42739CB00010B/2209